Nurturing
Your Blended
Family

Nurturing Your Blended Family

A Special Vocation

Ralph Ranieri

Liguori
ONE LIGUORI DRIVE
LIGUORI MO 63057-9999

Imprimi Potest:
Richard Thibodeau, C.Ss.R.
Provincial, Denver Province
The Redemptorists

Imprimatur:
Most Reverend Joseph F. Naumann
Auxiliary Bishop/Vicar General, Archdiocese of St.
Louis

ISBN 0-7648-1144-4
Library of Congress Catalog Card Number: 2003114442

To order, call 1-800-325-9521
www.liguori.org
www.catholicbooksonline.com

Dear Reader,

The book you hold in your hands is unique. While much of it talks about parenting children and step-children, and many of the examples given concern people who have divorced and remarried, the emphasis and overriding tone of this book is sacramental. The author stresses the importance of the sacramental graces of marriage, and the positive light in which the Church looks upon the families who are faithfully and diligently working at "blending"—becoming one when once they were two.

Tom Allender, a Jesuit priest who ministers to single-parent families, succinctly highlighted a societal problem that is by no means limited to single parents when he said: "Adults are finding it's easier to be a parent than a spouse" (quoted from *National Catholic Reporter* [8/29/03], "Hard times for families, couples, kids," by Arthur Jones). In a sense, what Fr. Tom is saying is that those parents who are not abusing or neglecting their children are doing just the opposite: they are investing themselves so totally into the kids that they are, in effect, abusing and neglecting their spouses. And then the marriage fails, and the kids grow up thinking whomever they marry will bow to their every wish just like Mom and Pop did. And then their marriage fails, and their kids grow up…well…you get the picture.

The author of this book is explicit: the marriage comes first. The best and most important gift you can *ever* give your children is to love each other. Two people in marriage are *already* a family without *any* children. The Second Vatican Council coined the phrase "domestic church," meaning two people loving each other in concert with God's love, living together in sacramental marriage. Every child that is added to the marital family extends and expands the domestic church outward, because love is contagious and the love of the couple is reflected in the children they raise—whether or not those children are bone of their bone and flesh of their flesh. Thus the vocation of marriage is a vocation that impacts *all* vocations, and the faithful work of blending two families into one is indeed a blessed work.

Illustrative of the extended blessing of blended families is this story: "Woman's liver donor is ex-husband" (St. Louis Post-Dispatch, 9/2/03), by Kaitlin Bell. The 32-year-old son of this divorced couple was a willing donor match, but he had recently suffered some serious injuries in an automobile accident. His mother couldn't wait much longer for a transplant. That's when the younger man's father—the ex-husband of the woman needing a transplant—stepped in. The man donated his liver to his ex-wife at the urging of his fiancée—who also provided comfort for all three adult children of the former couple during their ten long hours of surgery!

May you find blessing in this book, and may your blended family bathe in the graces of sacramental love.

The Editor

Contents

Introduction

In my thirty years as a social worker, I have worked with all kinds of families in every stage and age. I started out working with abused children, investigating their homes and sometimes sending them to foster homes or going to court on their behalf. I worked with parents who were raising children and coping with developmental problems. Presently I work with older families in a cancer center.

Of all the families I have worked with, one that I have had the most empathy for is the single-parent family. I know how much work there is in a two-parent family! I cannot imagine how these single parents raised children alone. Not only do they have to do twice the work, but also finances are always a problem. All the single mothers I saw were "working" mothers. Most of them worked very hard, and few made adequate money. Their benefits were poor and medical insurance was meager.

It was always a big day when single parents married. They were no longer alone. They now had a partner, not only to help with the work of raising a family but for emotional support. Most of the time, the new spouse had children of his or her own, so the family was increased in number, and everyone's role in the family changed. Parents went from the difficult position of "single" parent to the unique position of parent of a "blended" family. Whether they married someone with children or brought their own children into a new relationship, they now had to blend the new relationship or relationships into a harmonious family. This is no easy task. While their situation improved in many ways, these parent's role in the family became more complex.

I began to develop a new appreciation for people who take that daring step of not only giving marriage another chance, but of blending two families together. My admiration for the blended family grew just as it did for the single-parent family. I noticed that the "new" parent in a blended family needed to have a set of virtues uniquely his or her own—virtues different from those of a biological parent or single parent. The "new" parent in a blended family needed to be more fair than a biological parent, more willing to reach out, accepting of people from his or her spouse's past, and at times able to graciously handle rejection.

These parents in the blended family are unsung heroes of family life. They not only give themselves a second chance, but they give each other's children a second chance at family life. They marry, often quietly, and dive into their work. Sometimes they go unnoticed and unappreciated. Other times, they are looked on as second best—a stepparent. Our folklore, if you remember, has given stepparents a bad image. In many of these tales, like *Cinderella*, the adjective "wicked" preceded the word "stepmother."

Thank goodness, we have outgrown that little prejudice. But the stepparent still has to overcome the prejudices in his or her own family. The stepparent has to overcome what the stepchildren feel about him or her. He/she has to redefine him or herself to the children, not as a "replacement" for the biological parent, but as he or she chooses to be defined.

Stepparents across the country are doing this work, sometimes against all odds. I have written this book, first of all, to encourage them. I want to say to them, "Keep up the good work. The Church and the community need you." I don't feel that they get the credit or the support they deserve sometimes. Second, I have written this book in the hopes of being helpful. In some small way, I hope that I have written something or told a story in these pages that will give a partner in a blended family an idea of how to solve a problem, or maybe just a reason to persevere.

The sources for this work have been, first, my memory of thirty years of social work experience working with families. My own study and reading were also a major source. But my discussions with blended family members, priests, and counselors were my most important resources. They have made the writing come alive for me. Whenever I was bogged down, an interview with a blended family member would always fire me up and make me feel like I have got to tell this. All the names of people and places, of course, are changed; and the stories, while they describe one family, are often a composite of more than one family.

I have come to enjoy writing this book more than any other book I have written. I only hope it gives you a little encouragement and a bit of help.

Ralph Ranieri

Chapter One

Vocation

*S*hortly after graduation from a Catholic college, Ellen married Wes in the college chapel with seven of their priest friends from the faculty concelebrating the Nuptial Mass. Ellen had high expectations that everything she had ever dreamed about in marriage would come true in her marriage to Wes. She envisioned a quaint house, healthy children, and she and Wes supporting each other into old age. After eight years, Ellen had the house and the children, but she no longer had Wes.

They had arguments at first. The arguments led to grudges, and the grudges to long periods of stony silence. They grew further and further apart, until the marriage finally ended. Ellen and the children lived on their own. Wes went off to battle his own demons. Ellen found a good job, and supported herself and the children with sporadic help from Wes.

Then one day, when in her mid-thirties, Ellen met

another man. Dan was kind and good. He too had been through a first, troubled marriage, which had recently been annulled. Dan had wed his high school sweetheart in a small Methodist church that was pastored by her father. The union crumbled within three years.

Meeting Dan gave Ellen a spark of hope. In the back of her mind, she thought maybe she could have a happy family after all. Ellen sought, and obtained an annulment of her first marriage. Maybe God was giving not only her, but also Dan, a second chance. Eventually, Ellen and Dan married.

Like all marriages, whether they are the first or the second, the daily work of trying to make a relationship function smoothly began. Ellen not only worked on her relationship with Dan, but she also worked hard at her relationship with Dan's children. She was anxious to have them accept her. She worked with her own children, to help them acclimate to the new family. She wanted all the children to know that, just because this was a second marriage and everyone was not related by blood, it was no less a family than any other family. She also made it clear to the children that just because she and Dan had both had marriages that ended, it did not mean that this marriage was not starting out with a commitment to endure. "We are all in this together," Ellen told the family over and over. "We need to try to get along because we are all going to be here for several years. Dan and I are going to be in your lives even as grownups."

Ellen was wiser when she married Dan than when she married the first time. Her expectations were more appropriate. She was certainly more realistic about what could happen to a marriage. She prepared herself for things that were totally beyond her control. But even though she was realistic and aware, she still ran into many problems that she never faced before.

Dan had many relationships in his past—his first wife, children, former in-laws. Ellen had a long list of people in her life from the first marriage too. And she still had to learn the idiosyncrasies of the "new" children—who had a temper, who had allergies, who was Attention Deficit Disordered (ADD), who hated math. Ellen was wiser, but she had a host of problems that she needed to tackle—and they differed greatly from the problems newlyweds usually have to cope with.

God can make something good out of anything, even the demise of your first marriage. People who remarry after a divorce or death of a spouse and try to blend two families together have a very special vocation. This is not some "lesser opportunity." This is a *real* vocation—a chance to do God's will. This is a chance for two families to come together and heal, not only their own hurts, but also each other's hurts. It is an opportunity for two adults to bring children from two different families together—either on a part time or full time basis, depending on the custody arrangements—into a genuine family. Blood makes a family, like it or not; but you can make just as true a family out of love when no blood ties exist. A blended family comes together and provides this love for one another.

The premise of this book is that people who remarry and form a blended family have a special vocation, a sacramental vocation. The Church's annulment laws are an indication that the Church wants to be involved in blended families. The Church wants blended families involved in the life of the Church. The Church feels as though it can be of some help, and its annulment laws graciously allow for this. If they do not seem to in your particular case, that does not mean the Church does not want to be involved with you and your family. The laws on annulments are too complex to go into here, but do not presume you are on the outside. Speak to your pastor about your situation. And if you feel you were not understood by your pastor, find another priest to whom you can present your case.

Bringing people together in love is the greatest Christian work you can do on earth. To give yourself the way you give yourself in a family, and to attempt to blend two families into one, is an extraordinary Christian act. It puts you in a privileged situation. To be a part of bringing love and community to so many people who are not blood-related is a blessing.

When I was a student in social work, my professor asked us to write a paper describing one of the people we were working with at the time. I was working with a man at the VA Hospital who had just returned from Vietnam. Besides a leg wound, he suffered from a severe drug addiction. Since his return from Vietnam, he had difficulty holding a job. His wife left him. Then, shortly after leaving, his wife and young child were killed in a car accident.

I wrote the paper using my best style, trying to impress the professor. When he returned the paper to me, he had written on the back page in red ink: "You should consider it a privilege to have the opportunity to help a man who has had so much suffering in his life."

Those words hit me like a ton of bricks. I read them over and over. When I wrote the paper, I wasn't even thinking about the man's suffering; I was thinking about *my* grade!

My vocation crystallized in that moment. Social work is a vocation to help suffering people. And to do that on a daily basis, as part of your life's work, is indeed a privilege. Many vocations are a privilege, but *marriage* is a vocation that impacts *all* vocations, and *parenting* is the most important job in life. The late Jacqueline Kennedy said that if you bungle raising your children, none of your other accomplishments in life matter. The effects of our work as parents will reach further than anything else we do. The importance of the role of parent in a blended family is, obviously, just as important as it is in any other family.

What Is a Blended Family?

Just to make sure that we are all on the same page, let's define a "blended family." In a blended family, one or both spouses have children from a previous marriage. This husband and wife come together to form a new marriage. In so doing, they intend to blend two families into one. It makes no difference if some of the children spend time out of the "new" home with the former spouse, or if only one spouse has children. We still refer to this family as blended. The blended family also includes children that the couple may have together after marriage, as well as children who may be adopted and totally unrelated to either parent.

We need, also, to define "vocation." When people say they have a vocation, too many of us assume that they are going into the priesthood, or off to become a religious sister, or joining a group to do some specialized work like caring for lepers or the homeless. But two people who fall in love with one another also have a vocation. They are called together by God, to share their love in marriage, hopefully with children. This is a vocation—a call from God.

So what happens when two single parents fall in love? God may be calling them to a special vocation too. God may want them to share their love with each other's children and form a blended family. Just because these people are marrying for the second time, it does not mean that they do not have a vocation from God. Loving each other, and blending their children from a previous marriage into one family, may very well be their vocation.

Just read the Gospel carefully, and you will see that Jesus calls all kinds of people. He called the apostles, of course, and he called Zacchaeus down from a tree, and Lazarus from a tomb; he called the woman with a hemorrhage, the boy with the basket of fish, and Mary Magdalene after the Resurrection. God calls people in all ages to do all sorts of things. When the Church was becoming overwhelmed with power and authority, God called Benedict to show us how to live simply. When the Church was crumbling under its own accumulation of wealth, God called Francis of Assisi to show us the way to Christ-like poverty. Today, thirty percent of all our children are expected to spend part of their growing-up years in a step-family, or what we are calling here a blended family. It makes sense that God is calling previously-married men and women to lead these blended families.

Some people find that a vocation of caring for children and working with their problems comes quite naturally to them. I remember a young teacher who did an excellent job with children. She was organized and creative. When she married, she had two children of her own. Later, she and her husband adopted a child. That went so well that they adopted another. They moved to a bigger house, with acreage, and adopted children of many different races. Eventually, they had ten children in all. Their biological children, and those they adopted and blended into their family, all grew up healthy and well-adjusted.

Obviously, this teacher had a gift. You may have a gift and not even know it. A vocation is often manifested in a desire to do something. A man or woman who wants to enter the religious life has a desire to do so. A person who falls in love with someone who already has children has to discern whether he or she has the desire to not only be a spouse, but also a parent in a blended family. If one has the desire, and the situation seems fitting in all other respects, then we can say he/she has a vocation to be a spouse and a parent in a blended family.

Along with a vocation come special graces. This is just a theological way of saying that God gives us the tools to do the job. Just as one cannot go into the religious life without feeling a little awed, so too a person cannot enter a blended family without a sense of awe. That awe is there to remind us that we are not alone. The job is, of course, way over our heads, but in our vocation God promises us the grace—God's presence and love and help—to do the task at hand.

CHAPTER TWO

Family Adjustment

I once saw Jimmy and Rosalind Carter on a talk show. They were talking about the Carter Center and all that they had done since their retirement. They had gone from the highest profile job in the world to working in their home office, which was a converted garage. Jimmy was saying that one of the things he and Rosalind "will never do again" is write a book together. One author makes a good deal of changes when writing a book. I can only imagine how many changes two authors make, and then they have to agree on the changes!

Change is difficult for all of us. When two adults and a group of children go from a nuclear family to a blended family, the changes can sometimes shatter a few nerves and cause children to react in ways that parents are not used to. One definition of "crisis" is a situation in which your normal, everyday coping mechanisms no longer work. Divorce is a crisis.

Likewise, blending a family can create a crisis for one or more of its members. People begin to act in ways that are not normal for them. They are trying to cope, but the usual coping mechanisms are not working. One guidance counselor told me that he has found it is far more difficult for girls to be away from their fathers than it is for boys. He did not know of any particular reason for this, but he said it was a consistent problem in his groups.

Problems can start right from the beginning. The custodial parent usually ends up bearing the brunt of the anger. The child perceives the custodial parent as the one who is to blame for the other parent not being there. Now, the child also blames the custodial parent for the presence of this new spouse. If a child has an axe to grind, the custodial parent is the grindstone. That's why as much preparation as possible is needed, so that the children can ready themselves for this change.

John had been dating Carol for several weeks. The two of them would often go out and take their children with them. They would go to nature parks, the beach, or out to eat. John realized it was important to pay attention to Carol's daughter, so he spoke to her often. He asked her questions about school, and when they went to amusement parks, he took her on rides. His son did not seem to mind this, because John also paid a good deal of attention to the boy.

This seemed an ideal relationship for a while. Then

things began to break down. It wasn't intentional, but it seemed that everyone started taking each other for granted. As time went on, John paid what he deemed was a "normal" amount of attention to Carol's daughter. He figured he had won her over, that now they had a relationship he could relax with. John no longer went out of his way to give her exorbitant amounts of his time.

Soon, Carol's daughter began to have problems. "He used to pay attention to me, but he doesn't anymore," she told her mother. John was completely in the dark about what was going on.

Sometimes, the problem can be the adult's. A new spouse may feel that he or she is not getting enough attention because all the effort is going into helping the children adjust. The problem of attention comes in many forms and many sizes. We all want attention, at whatever age, and when we are in a whole new situation, like a blended family, we need extra assurance that we are loved. Such assurance usually comes in the form of attention, and if we do not get that attention, we can start to show symptoms of insecurity.

Let's take Mark, whose mother married a man that had custody of his own children on weekends. Mark's routine was upset. At least that is the way he explained it. He complained about sharing space—but what Mark was truly upset about was sharing his mother. He did not feel like he received enough attention when his stepbrother was visiting. His mother, in his opinion, seemed to go overboard in giving attention to her husband's son.

Mark did not act out in school. He did not get into any trouble, but he had quieter problems. He complained about not being able to concentrate, and he was withdrawn. When children withdraw, their problems are harder to pick up than when they act out. When a child becomes overly quiet, that can be the sign of a problem.

What's the answer? From what others tell me, and from what I have seen in my own experiences, the answer lay in how the child's biological parents get along. Even though the problem may not *seem* to involve the absent biological parent, that parent is imminently important. How the separated biological parents get along with one another creates an atmosphere for the blended family. Even though the child may live with his mother and stepfather, what determines his mood the most is how well his biological parents relate to one another.

When a boy's father takes him home after a day out, and the boy's mother comes out to greet his dad and say hello, that makes all the difference in the world to the child. When the two biological parents talk civilly in front of their child, that has a positive effect. It makes the child feel that there is still a connection between the two people he loves.

This does not have to be unrealistic. The child may know that he is the only reason his parents are talking to each other, but when they are in harmony it makes him feel better. It can help the child deal with underlying problems, like a perceived lack of attention in his blended home. Rather than feeling shut out, he feels included when his parents are at least cooperative. It makes the adjustment to the blended family easier for him.

"My parents get along better now than when they were married," one child said. Children notice the difference in the way their parents get along. If they do get along better after the divorce—which is really the purpose of the divorce—the child seems to do better. Constant parental bickering after the divorce seems to be one of the things that has the most dramatic effect on a child. Complaining about a lack of attention may simply be a symptom of the child's distress over his or her two biological parents not getting along.

Children have a way of knowing when they are being used. They know that, if they are being quizzed about their father's marriage or their mother's relationship, their biological parents are on hostile ground. Questions should never be asked of the children regarding your ex-spouse, nor should children ever be used as messengers. Communicate directly with one another if this is possible.

If the biological parents are getting along, it makes it easier when a new parent comes into the family. A calm atmosphere is like oil in a machine; it keeps things running smoothly. I know one child psychiatrist who is always insisting upon tranquility in dealing with troubled children. That might sound funny, because troubled children create everything *but* tranquility. But he believes that, if you keep the atmosphere calm, the child has a better chance of staying calm or returning to a calm state. An angry or hysterical atmosphere only excites the child emotionally.

A calm atmosphere between biological parents also helps a child to accept his or her stepparent. If the situation is neutral between the biological parents, the child will not see the stepparent in a competitive light. When there seems to be competition, the child feels forced to take sides, or feels guilty for choosing one parent over the other.

It is *always* important that children be free from guilt over a divorce. The divorce should be explained in terms of Mommy and Daddy not getting along. No one else, including the children, has anything to do with it. A child can feel bad for his or her parents, but he/she has to realize that their divorce is their problem. The child did not cause it; neither can he/she fix it.

One mother of a blended family told me: "I always wait. If communication breaks down with my ex-husband or former mother-in-law, I wait. I never force a situation. You get nothing accomplished that way. I wait. Things usually open up if you look for an opportunity."

Patience is the key. You and your ex-spouse may

not get along all the time, on all subjects, but do not carry things over to the next encounter. Be patient. Try to start over after a disagreement. Or, better yet, drop the subject when it gets volatile, and come back to it later.

Both children and spouses are making a major adjustment when they start a blended family. Think of the task that two stepparents have when, for the first time, they have to come together with their children. A young mother of a blended family said to me: "After you introduce them, then what? Do you tell them, 'All right, kids, you'd better get along, because we are all going to live together till you're adults'? No, you don't say that, but there have been plenty of times when I sat everybody down and told them that the only way we are going to make it is *if* we all get along. So we have to get along."

Sometimes the children will bond easily. They have all been through a similar loss, grief, and separation; they want peace too. A *Christian Science Monitor* report (4/3/02) told of one blended family where both parents had a seventh- and an eighth-grader. The mother said that you usually don't get two eighth-graders or two seventh-graders from the same family. They really grew to depend on one another. If they moved to a new place, they had each other as "built-in-buddies." While they were making friends, and even after they made new friends in their new school, they always had each other.

The *Monitor* article also said that children can

learn valuable lessons in step-families. Watching their parents go through a divorce, kids become aware of a wide variety of emotions. Then, in learning to live with new family members, they acquire coping skills and the ability to adjust to change early in life. Of course, it does not always happen so smoothly, but it is nice to know that if the child is up to it, positive things can happen.

I know a woman who never misses an opportunity to point out things for her kids to learn, even from negative experiences. If the children complain about a teacher, the mother says that maybe the teacher's baby was sick and she was worried. If a child is upset about his poor performance in a soccer game, she reminds him of what the great quarterback Charlie Ward said after a close loss to Notre Dame: "Nobody died." If a receptionist or store clerk is impatient with them, she says maybe the clerk's boss is giving her a hard time. She wants her children to know that people do not act in an impatient manner just because they are mean, and that disappointments have to be put into perspective. Understanding other people's emotions helps children understand their own. Going through a divorce, and moving into a blended family, gives children ample opportunity to understand people's emotions—and consequently their own.

I have heard some professionals go so far as to suggest that when a blended family starts out, they ideally should buy a new house. The new house is neutral territory. Certainly, the idea has some merit, but it is also impractical. So much change is already going on that it might help the new family more if they don't have to move. Moving is one of the most stressful things you can do. Healing feelings from the previous marriage is important for children, and it may not be as easy for them as it is for adults. If kids can stay in their own house, in their own room, the atmosphere for healing will at least be less stressful. Obviously, *somebody* will have to move, in order for the blended family to be together, but keep change in mind. The less changes you have to make for yourself and the children, the better.

After marriage, the stepparent takes on a different role in the children's eyes, and everyone needs to understand that role. This is not going to happen in one sit-down conversation, of course. This is a vocation, remember, and it has to be worked at in cooperation with God's grace. It may take many talks and constant explanations. It is one thing to say, "I know"; it is entirely something else to actually experience and feel the reality of a situation and accept it. That takes time with everyone, especially the kids. Give them the time they need to let what they "know" get from their heads to their hearts. The only way to do that is to try to relax and let the relationships take their natural course.

"When I first got married, I felt I was out of my element," a stepmother told me. "I was twenty-seven. I had a stepchild thirteen-years old. This was my first marriage. I wanted to please my husband by making his child happy. I wanted to please everyone. But it was only after I began to relax that the relationship with my stepson began to grow. It has never stopped growing. We are still friends today, and he's a grown man who calls me 'Mom.'"

The same woman said that she never insisted the boy call her Mom. "It isn't fair to make a child with a biological mother in another part of town call you 'Mom,'" she said. This boy called his stepmother by her first name for quite some time. Eventually, he decided on his own to call her "Mom." You have to find a name that everyone is comfortable with, and use it. If or when the child wants to call you "Mom," it should be his or her decision.

Age-level Characteristics

According to counselors, younger children have an easier time adjusting to a blended family. Children of preschool age need closeness, and a healthy blended family simply absorbs them; the young child needs the family, and the family is eager to have the child.

Adolescents, on the other hand, may have a more difficult time. They are old enough to understand the finality of divorce, but not quite mature enough to understand all the reasons for it, so their response is often anger that is hard to deal with because it is not specific. Some adolescents, however, are already beginning to separate from the family; they seem to have less emotional investment in the blended family, as their focus is on their own interests and relationships.

The kids that seem to have the most trouble adjusting are the middle-school group. They are old enough to know what is going on, and they still have six or seven years left in the family. They can be angry or depressed. Withdrawal is one of the ways in which many show their anger and depression, as opposed to acting out or getting into conflicts. They often say things like, "I can't concentrate." This is reflected in poor grades. When the children act out their anger, the problem is of course more obvious. They may have conflicts with the teachers or with their classmates, and these conflicts can be physical or verbal.

Teens need equal amounts of acceptance and explanations. Even when they do not want an explanation, it may help to give them one. Guidance is still necessary for teens. Sometimes parents let go too early and too completely. You may be tempted to feel your job with your teen is over because you already have your hands full with younger children and you are trying to make adjustments to your new marriage. But stay with it a little bit longer. Don't let go too soon. Don't make an *almost* independent adult feel as though his or her independence is being rushed because of your remarriage. Teens still need to know they belong.

Whatever the age, and whether the child's

problem is displayed through withdrawal or acting out, you need to get involved in this. It is good to let teachers know that your child is going through a divorce or an adjustment to a blended family. If talking to your child about problems does not seem to help, do not be timid about going to a professional counselor. Start with the school. See if they have any suggestions. I can tell you from personal experience that you may not find the right counselor immediately. You may have to look, try, and ask repeatedly, but do not quit. A good counselor can be a great help in these situations, not only to the child, but also to the parents. He or she may give you the added strength and encouragement you need to go on.

I know a mother who helped her daughter because she did not give up when she ran into dead-ends and poor service organizations. She kept searching, and finally found a doctor who understood the girl and her problem. Help is out there. Look for it. It is always more supportive if you and your spouse agree that the child can use some professional help.

I started this book by saying that spouses in a blended family have a special vocation. However, vocations are not necessarily easy. What makes them possible is that we can always count on the grace of God to help us in difficult situations.

CHAPTER THREE

Putting Your
Heads Together

*H*e lived alone with two daughters. One of them was seriously ill and needed a lot of his attention, sometimes immediately. He had to change jobs so he could be close to home. He managed it well, surprising himself. As coincidence would have it, he met a single mother at his new job. She also had two daughters, roughly the same ages as his daughters. They often compared notes about the trials and tribulations of single parenthood. They found a support in each other.

One day, he had to go out of town unexpectedly. He asked her if she could watch his two children. "Sure," she said. "What are two more?" He gave her the medicine for his sick child, told her how to use it, and went off to the train station.

All day long, he worried about how the kids were

doing. Was it too much to ask her to do? His children could be difficult at times, and he hoped that they were not giving her a hard time.

His fears vanished when he returned home and found that, not only did his friend survive, but also everyone had a nice day. "The kids really got along well," she said.

You are probably one step ahead of me here. The two parents fell in love. Both of them felt an unfinished need in terms of family. "If my first marriage had stayed together, I would have liked two more children," she said. "Now I have them."

Throughout the courtship, the children remained friends. When it came time for the marriage, the children could not wait to move in together. They were close friends, and now they wanted to be family. The two parents had a great relationship and kids were getting along. What a great start!

What does this marriage have to teach us? It teaches that *cooperation is essential*. In a blended family, cooperation is a matter of life and death. If people do not cooperate, or try to cooperate with one another, things fall apart very quickly. Cooperation is necessary even when the team does not want to cooperate. I want you to see that family life, whatever the makeup, takes an extraordinary amount of work. I know of no perfect marriages. I don't even know of a normal marriage, if what is meant by "normal" is a marriage without problems.

We learn from this family the importance of helping each other, especially with decisions. Here's what
happened in this well-adjusted blended family. The
oldest daughter, the father's biological daughter, decided she wanted to try living with her mother. That
meant she would have to leave the blended family,
and this was a number of years after the marriage.
Understandably, this caused a stir in the family. The
first question the family had to tackle was whether this
would be a positive move for the girl. The family was
concerned, both the kids and the parents. But the parents felt like they had to let their daughter try. She went
away, and they really missed her.

The important lesson here is that when bolts come
out of the blue, you should not try to handle them
alone. The two parents in the blended family shared
this decision. They shared the worry. But they coop-
erated on it. It was a tough decision, made easier
because of their mutual involvement and their mutual agreement.

We learn the need to cooperate on discipline. What
happened here was that the mother in the blended
family tried to take care of all the discipline herself.
The role seemed to come easier to her, and she just
assumed it. She found, however, that it could not work
that way. "I was even-handed, and I even did back
flips to make sure that I was no harder on his children than on mine," she said, "but the biological parent has so much influence."

One of the husband's biological teenage children

suddenly began to fail in school. At first, the step-mother helped her with her lessons. Then she tried to discipline her. No results. Finally, she went to her husband. "You've got to do something to help me."

The father stepped up to the plate. He told the girl that if the grades didn't improve she would not be leaving the house next semester. Everyone was surprised at the power the father had. Even he was surprised! Up came the grades, almost as if this is what the girl was waiting for.

I have heard this over and over again from step-parents. They tell me that, ideally, the biological parent has to be involved regardless of whether he/she is in the home or not.

Let me give you another example.

A mother's college-age biological daughter started to give her some static about not returning to college. The mother felt it was a manipulation. The mother tried everything to get her daughter to return to college. As a last resort, the woman called her former husband. Their relationship was fair, depending on the issue. "You've got to help me. She's refusing to go back to college for no good reason," the mother said.

The father lived five hours away in Miami. His response surprised his ex-wife. "You tell her to have her bags packed, because I am coming up there personally and taking her back to school in Georgia." The mother relayed that message to her daughter—and she packed her bags.

The mother said that this is not only the power of the biological parent, but also the power of everybody being on the same page. You have to agree on values, and you have to agree to do all that is necessary to enforce or salvage your values. Both parents in the blended family and the out-of-house biological parent agreed on this one. This certainly helps to make a child feel loved.

But the mother insists that she still disciplines and advises her stepchildren. "A therapist told me once that I could not discipline my stepchildren. It was a mistake to listen to him," she said. "One time I did not step in when my stepchild needed me, and I think she felt like I abandoned her. Now I discipline, but I include their father."

Another thing we learn about cooperation from our "model" family is how to face outside interference. Stick together—whether the interference comes from society in general or from the extended family. The mother of this family said that one evening, when she was single-parenting, she went out on a date. The man came to the house to pick her up and he met her children. Once they were seated in the restaurant, he said to her, "I did not know you had luggage."

"Of course I do," she said. "I travel for business. Don't you have luggage?"

"No," he said, "luggage—like in children."

She says it was a short date!

Some people consider children an impediment for a single person. Other people think going into a marriage with kids from two families is way too much work. "'You're crazy,' is what my friends told me," she said. "You think you can parent someone else's kids? Look at how hard it is to parent your own." She went on to say, "I know at least one marriage counselor who advised a couple not to marry until their kids were in their twenties."

When the support is not coming naturally from society, the husband and wife of the blended family have to stick together. And these two did. They knew exactly what they were doing. They agreed on it, and they worked toward it.

But interference can also come from the family.

After a visit to her biological mother, one child told her stepmother, "My mommy does not like you." A little taken aback, the stepmother finally said, "I don't feel that way about your mommy." She wasn't sure why she had said that, but she felt that it was important for the children to know there was not a war going on in the family. The stepmother said that sometimes it is hard when one of the biological parents will tell the kids, "Your mother [or father] should not do" this or that. You have to calmly tell the children that everybody has a different way of doing things, and some things can be done a million different ways.

The stepparents I spoke to are unanimous on this one. *Never* talk badly about the biological parent, no matter what. If you do, it will come back to haunt you.

But the children love it when you get along.

Some years ago, the mother of the ex-husband in our family had some seriously negative words with the biological mother of this family. The biological mother, of course, was hurt, but now the children will come home from a visit and say, "Grandma was asking for you. Call her, please." She sees how happy it makes them, so she calls and chats amiably while the children listen and smile. What she learned is that, when dealing with grandparents who are ex-in-laws, there is more at stake than whether or not you personally like the people. You represent not only yourself, but also your children and your whole blended family.

"You have to stick together to make peace and security exist," the stepmother says. "One of the things we never do is to put the other parent down. You have to decide the kind of family you want, and then go about making it."

Another lesson in cooperation: Cooperation means trying to love all the kids equally. If the husband and the wife are going to cooperate, they must be fair and just in their treatment of all the children. When the stepmother in this family tried to tell some of her friends that her goal was to treat all the children equally, they responded with statements like, "You are robbing your own kids of your love."

"This isn't necessarily so," says the stepmother. "Since when does loving another person mean you love someone else less? The more love in the environment, the more love to go around. I think my children like it when all things are equal. They feel bad when things are unfair. If one of their relatives brings them a gift without bringing something for their step-siblings they feel embarrassed," the mother said. "What gets a little sticky is when you are out with your stepdaughter, trying to buy her a prom dress or something, she might say, 'Why can't my mom do this for me?' My standard reply is, 'Honey, if she was here she would.'"

No matter how equal you try to be, sometimes you cannot help feeling emotionally different about your own children. That is nothing to be ashamed of. It is natural. Just try to be fair with all of them.

Sometimes you are instinctively defensive about your own child.

"I cooked a big meal," the stepmother told me. "Everyone was expected home for dinner. I had all this food ready, and my husband tells me his daughter went out to a party and would not be home for dinner. 'She knew I was cooking dinner,' I said. 'Why did she do that?'

"My husband started to defend her. 'It was a last minute thing. A friend came by.' I saw what was happening and let it drop."

She says that in the beginning she did the same thing. But as time has passed, both parents have become more objective. "We both try to keep it balanced, and not blame each other's children or get too defensive about our own."

This family took a giant step in terms of cooperation when the oldest child graduated from high school
and the family had a party at their house. The husband and wife invited everyone, and everybody
came—their ex-spouses with their new spouses, the
in-laws, and the former in-laws. They were all there,
and everybody had a wonderful time. The happiest
people in the group were the children.

Love is patient. Love is kind. Love is also cooperative. So much in a blended family calls for cooperation. All of our past relationships need to be respected. All the children need respect. And, like every marriage, blended or not, husband and wife must
be respectful and accepting of each other, especially
in their differences. Cooperation is the key.

CHAPTER FOUR

Discipline

"Come into the house," a father calls.

"No," shouts a four-year-old boy.

The father steps out of the house, and off the little fellow runs. Especially with his head start, the father has a hard time catching up to the lad. The child screams loudly enough, while he runs, to embarrass the father. So the father abandons the chase. Slowly, the little boy begins to wander home.

When the child eventually gets home, what happens is discipline. Discipline is how we teach our children to control their emotions, to obey rather than follow a whim. It is something that must take place in every family. It is a part of parental vocation. That parent has a tough job ahead of him when the little runaway finally gets home.

Imagine the scene above from a different perspective. Suppose it was the child's stepfather who called him into the house and the child yelled, "No." What

31

should the stepfather do? Call the mother to take care of it? Go out after the child himself? Or just forget about it?

Let's suppose he does the same thing the other father did—he goes out after the child. Suppose the child takes off screaming. He's in the same predicament as the biological father was—embarrassed to be chasing a screaming child down the street. Now what does the stepfather do?

The difference between what the biological father did and what the stepfather will do is that *what the stepfather does has to be predetermined.* In other words, the child's mother has to have given the stepfather a role, and the child has to know that role. In families where only the biological parent makes the decisions and calls the shots, the stepparent is left in a powerless position.

A stepparent should never try to replace a biological parent, but he or she must have some control over a situation, especially if the biological parent is not present. The most confusion comes in families where the biological parent does everything. Then, when the stepparent needs to step in, he or she is met with, "You're not my father [or mother]." But if the family has discussed roles beforehand, the child knows that the stepparent is a genuine authority figure who must be obeyed and respected, just as the child's "real" parent is.

Stepparents need to understand their role in the family, including what is expected of them in terms of parental discipline. A biological mother once told me that her daughter was planning to return to her biological father and his new wife. The mother did not think it was a good idea, and she told the daughter why. The stepfather was silent on the issue. "Come on," the biological mother said, "get involved in this or she will think you don't care where she lives." So the stepfather told her why he thought she should stay with them. He did not make any negative remarks about the girl's father in his rationale for wanting her to stay put.

None of this was sufficient for causing the girl to change her mind, but it helped nonetheless. She later said that she was glad her stepfather cared enough to tell her so, and to do it in a manner wholly respectful of both her and her biological father.

Stepparenting is an art more than a science. You intervene when you feel it is right to, and you refrain for the same reasons. You'll occasionally step into the wrong situation, but everybody does that. Certainly, biological parents sometimes could do better with their kids. Older children, especially, are adept at baiting parents into arguments; and parents should never ask questions of their kids that they really do not want to know the answers to. You have your spouse to help you balance your feelings, and to tell you whether or not you should get involved in a particular parental problem. You need to help each other out, and work together on discipline.

This is probably as good a place as any to bring

up the subject of loyalty. While the biological parent and the stepparent are trying to make the best of their situation, the child's absent parent continues to play a huge role in their family. Children have unseen ties of loyalty that bind them to their absent parent. You may not even know what they consider loyalty until you run into a stone wall of belligerence from them, and even then, you may not know the real meaning of what is going on. If it is shortly after a visit to the out-of-house parent that your child acts out against you, for example, you may feel that the absent parent betrayed you somehow. Perhaps he or she said something negative about you. But that is not necessarily so. The child may have his or her own reasons for suddenly deciding to make a stand for loyalty, and those reasons may seem to you to be unreasonable. Tread carefully here.

When nothing else makes sense—when children cannot come up with a reasonable explanation for their actions, when they do not seem to know what they want, when they contradict themselves—loyalty issues become suspect. The child's thoughts are a jumble to him/her, and he/she cannot explain them very well. Nevertheless, they are extremely important to the child, and they must be treated as important.

Try bringing up the issue of loyalty with the rebellious child. Perhaps you can help him or her to understand that what you are doing within this new relationship is not a betrayal to his/her biological parent, nor does the child's separation from that parent make him/her any less loyal. You might explicitly say, "No one would ever want you to be less loyal to your father [or mother]."

This is an almost inevitable built-in pain that a blended family experiences from time to time. If you consider that loyalty issues are expressions of grief on the child's part, you may be able to understand them better and deal with them more effectively.

Jennifer did not understand all the reasons for her parents' divorce, but in the back of her mind, she thought her father was the victim. Jennifer lived with her mother, and whenever she visited her father he seemed melancholy. In Jennifer's mind, her father's mood stemmed from the divorce. She began to reason that the divorce was her mother's fault. "If Mom would only take him back, we can all be happy again," she told herself. When this did not happen, Jennifer began to give her mother the "cold shoulder." She did not talk to her mother unless it was absolutely necessary. She declined to go shopping or visiting when her mother invited her to come along. This was all because Jennifer thought that her mother was making her father unhappy.

When her mother remarried, the door was slammed shut on Jennifer's fantasy of reconciliation between her biological parents. In Jennifer's mind, the stepfather became one of the culprits in her father's unhappiness. Jennifer continued her passive-aggressive behavior, and acted very coolly toward her new stepfather and his daughter. When he tried to communicate with her, Jennifer's explanation of how she felt was convoluted, confusing, and hard to follow. Fortunately, the stepfather was sensitive enough to know that when a child is confused, it might mean the child is dealing with issues that he or she is unsure about revealing. The stepfather acted friendly and accepting, and was complimentary to the girl's father.

Jennifer could not help her feelings. She loved her father, and hated to see him sad. That made her sad, and she displayed her emotions in anger. But thanks to the understanding of her mother and stepfather, her feelings were eventually neutralized.

In time, her father also remarried. His sadness lifted, and Jennifer had a more congenial relationship in the home.

Children will be watching the stepparent for signs of loyalty to his or her biological children. Children are sticklers for fairness, and anything that creates an unfair environment in their eyes needs to be improved. In most of the blended families I have known, the children generally get along well. They are not looking to pick a fight with each other. But they do want fairness all the way around. They expect it from their stepparent, and they even expect their biological parent to be fair to their step-siblings.

One mother told me how she took her two girls

and her two stepdaughters shopping for school. She tried to be fair. She tried to get everybody what they needed without showing any partiality. Did her children feel slighted? "Not at all," she says, "that is what they expected."

"Once my father came to the house," the mother continued, "and he had gifts for my two girls and nothing for my stepchildren. I could tell the my girls felt bad, and they immediately proceeded to share the two gifts with their stepsisters."

Most of the time, children are impressed with the way their parents show love to others. They rarely feel like anything is being taken away from them. Most of the time, however, the behavior that is presented to the stepparent is different from what the biological parent gets. The biological parents are the ones who usually hold the power, even though they may not be present in the home. Just as the child has to learn how to accept the authority of the stepparent, the stepparent has to accept the fact that, even though he/she might be loved and respected, he/she may never become number one in the children's eyes.

One man could not understand how his stepdaughter could favor her biological father over him. He had done so much for her. He had practically raised her. Her biological father never paid support, and often did not show up for visits, leaving the girl disappointed over and over. What this stepfather did not understand is that biological favoritism is seldom a logical conclusion that kids come to; it is strictly an emotional conclusion. Learn to accept it.

A part of vocation is putting in lots of time and sacrifice, and often without getting all the return you deserve. At times when we are frustrated by that, we have to remember the good work we are doing. Both stepparents and biological parents have a duty to the children. Neither one of them can afford to look around and determine whether they are getting what they think they "deserve."

Sometimes, however, loyalty issues may not be innocent and natural. Jan Anderson, in "Challenges of the Stepfamily" (www.mothersover40.com), feels the biggest problem she ran into was propaganda spread by the children's biological mother. This mother often asked the children to spy on Anderson, to see what kind of work she was doing at home. When Anderson realized this, she had to accept the fact that some problems were beyond her control.

However, Anderson did take action when she felt it necessary. When loyalty issues caused the children to treat her rudely in her husband's absence, she told him about it upon his return. He then spoke to the children about it. Anderson felt that it was important for everyone to know that they were responsible for polite behavior regardless of who they were with.

It has been my experience that all things even out. Children will realize that you care for them. If they are asked to do things like "spy on you," they will realize that is wrong too. The children eventually understand well-meaning stepparents, and even in-terfering biological parents, in the long run. The short run may produce misunderstandings, but they do not last.

Discipline does not have to be hard, but it needs to be there. It is the behavior that we are responsible for as adults and children. Discipline, essentially, is a teaching tool. In a blended family, who is supposed to be the teacher may be blurred at times. That needs to be made clear, no matter how many explanations it takes.

The kind of disciplinarian you are will have a great deal to do with the kind of personality you have. You can't force yourself to discipline like someone else. You have to be yourself. But you must have a clear role. The biological parent must make sure that all the children understand the authority of the steppar-ent. Only in this way can you be a better teacher to your children.

CHAPTER FIVE

The Ties That Bind

When the family "blends," everyone is happy. When the family is hurt, everybody in the family bleeds from the same emotional artery. Two people in the family fall into conflict, and all grow tense. No member can escape anything that happens in the family. No matter how insignificant it is, it affects the whole. You can never say, "I don't care because it doesn't concern me." It always concerns you—even if you just think about it or wonder about it or ponder what might have happened if you did care. The family has a way of making its members one organism, even though they remain individuals. The children are an extension of the oneness of the spouses, a part of the marital vocation. What is it that binds all together into one? It isn't blood. It is caring, concern, and love. That is why you are always affected by what happens. And when you care, sometimes you worry.

Nobody escapes worry. While we are here on earth, we are still trying to trust God and let go of things. Most of us can do this in varying degrees. But because we are imperfect, we cannot do it completely, so we worry. Part of being a parent or stepparent means you worry. I know people in their seventies and eighties, and they still worry about their children and grandchildren. They worry about their children's health, their happiness, their marriages. These aren't obsessive worriers, but people with normal, day-to-day worries, such as: Will our kids "make it"—socially? academically? Will they avoid peer pressure? Will they get over this marital hurdle? Worry is part of the sacrifice we all make as parents. No matter how great our faith, no matter how deep our trust, we worry. Trust in God helps us handle it.

How many parents, down through the years, have sat up at night—reading the Bible, praying the rosary, or watching old movies on TV—waiting for a fifteen- or sixteen-year-old to come home? Worry goes with the territory. I've sat up many nights watching *The Hunt for Red October*. It is my "worry movie," the one that seems to distract me the best.

A little bit of worry is natural. It goes along with the physical exertion and exhaustion that comes from family work. At times we feel like we should get a medal for it, but it's all a part of the job of parenting. I look at some of the young parents I work with and remember what it was like. I can see the exhaustion in their eyes at the end of the day, but I know that they go home to no rest. They will pick the children up from the baby sitter or day care, and the children will be rearing to go. Tired or not, they have to parent.

If the children do not live with you, you may have added worries about them. Depending upon how often you see them, you may wonder how they are doing. When an older teenage boy decided that he was going to live with his father, his mother and stepfather had some concerns. He was doing well in school, and playing on the basketball team, which meant so much to him. They wondered how he would make the transition to a new school and a new home. They were also worried about his biological father making the transition. He did not seem too enthusiastic about his son's coming.

Every family has worries, but this is the kind of thing that causes a little extra worry in a blended family. The stepfather of the boy said, "It takes a hearty soul to do this job, and it takes a lot of trust in God. I don't know how I would get along if I could not put things in God's hands." He was referring, among other things, to the fact that they still had children at home demanding their attention while they were worrying about the absent son.

But whether it is worry or work, you are not alone. Look around you. It is no different in most families. They are all struggling constantly to make the children feel as connected as possible.

I guess that we all review our interactions with the children in our minds, over and over. I know that

I am a great second-guesser. When something goes wrong, I keep wondering what I could have done differently. One of the best ways to cope with worry is to talk to other parents, ideally, parents in a blended family situation. Community does not take away the problems, but it does put them into perspective; and it takes away the feeling that we are all alone and uniquely afflicted.

One person was telling me how badly his family felt because their house was so crowded. The blended family had filled their house to overflowing. When the parents spoke to another couple who had exactly the same problem, they felt a lot better. It did not give them any more room in their house, but it helped them to realize that they were not the only parents in the world who subjected their children to a little crowding, and that everyone would survive it.

The people in your own family also provide a good place to get support and find some relief from everyday problems. Most blended families could use some relaxation. Make sure your family gets some recreation together. Playing together is a good bonding force for relationships. It is often easier to talk about things when all are relaxed and away from their everyday environment too. Members are not so defensive, and no one is apt to feel left out.

One of the things I have observed about the blended families I have met is how fluidly they interact. It's impossible to distinguish them from a biologically-intact family. In most blended families, one can't tell who the biological parent is and who the stepparent is. A family is not meant to be self-conscious. Allow yourself to be yourself. Welcoming a child into the family is a natural act. It will come naturally to you. It may not come as easily to the child who will need time to adjust.

Time is of the essence with children. If you remember that children need time to enter into relationships, you can cut your worry in half. Just remind yourself, whenever you are having a minor problem, that they need time. In some ways, of course, children are more flexible than adults because they do not have the ingrained habits of adults. But while this lack of experience might make them flexible, it also sometimes makes them slow to develop habits. We need to give children the time they need to relate to us. We cannot rush relationships with children.

Consistency helps. If a person is insincere, children will pick it up. How many times have children been uncomfortable around the same people you were uncomfortable with? They may not be able to explain it, but they know it. Don't let worry make you rush headlong into relationships and forget that they take time. It is always better to be a little distant, but sincere, than to try to move too close too fast.

You can avoid a lot of worry about the relationship if you use the resources around you. Talk to your spouse about the children. Talk to the absent biological parent about the children. You need to learn so much about these children and their personalities!

Do not think this is something that you can figure out all by yourself. When those who have lived with the children all their lives surround you, they can be your best allies.

A stepmother told me that she learned a lot about the children from their biological mother. She did not have a chummy relationship with the children's mother, but she listened. She once mentioned a particular problem that she was having with one of the kids, and the biological mother said, "That one is an independent spirit." That struck a chord in the stepmother. That's exactly what the child was! She thought to herself, "I am going to have to back off and not be so surprised when this one does not jump at my suggestions."

More ideally, the stepparent can learn a lot about the children from his/her spouse. This is a close and willing source that should be utilized. Listen. Talk to one another about the children. Make it a team effort. Support each other, especially with a difficult child. This can cut down on your anxieties and on potential problems.

This is what one stepfather learned from talking to his wife about a problem relationship with his stepson: "Johnny's ADD gives him more problems than just not being able to sit still. He can't stay on a task very long. He does not like long conversations, and has trouble with eye contact. But he can play anything with you all day long. That's the best time to talk to him—while you are playing."

In another conversation, a biological parent revealed to her new spouse, "If you make my daughter feel guilty, no matter how justified you are, she will become angry and stop talking."

Little tips from the biological parent help a stepparent not only to relate better, but also to not become discouraged. Husbands and wives reminding each other that they are doing a good job, and not to take things too seriously, gives much needed support to fledgling stepparents. We need to be reassured in many of the jobs we do. The work we do in our blended family is extremely important, and sometimes we are treading on unfamiliar ground. Support is essential.

Alfred Adler, one of the great contemporaries of Sigmund Freud, said that one of the best antidotes for anxiety is to not feel alone. In a family, we should make every effort to make sure that no one ever feels alone. When we feel a relationship growing, and trust being established, worry lessens. Worry may never go away completely, but it does decrease. After a while, as we witness our family blossoming, we will understand that a little worry is a small price to pay for the momentous privilege of blending a family.

CHAPTER SIX

Anger

A human emotion that most of us dislike and few of us completely control is anger. The blended family needs to be always aware of anger. If you are not angry, be careful that the actions and words of angry children in the blended family, or the words and actions from your former family, don't make you angry. Depending upon how relationships were left in your former family, your ex-spouse or his/her family, could create angry situations for you. Remember that anger hurts the one who is angry the most. The majority of people that you may be angry with probably don't even know it.

Divorce always has some anger in it. Even if it was an amicable divorce, you may be angry about things not working out as planned, the way you were treated, the way the children were treated, and the settlement. There can be many reasons for anger, and they can express themselves in many ways. There is a school of psychology that likes to get into all those hurts and dwell on them. Sometimes, you may have to do that, but most of the time, the sooner you can let go of the bad feelings, the better it is for you. Just tell yourself that you handled everything that was bad for you by getting out of it. You do not have to do any more than that. You do not have to get revenge, or get even. Life is too short for that. Leaving a bad situation is enough.

What you need to do is get on with your life. Anger lingers if you have nothing to replace it with. When you get involved with something else—your family, a job, a cause, your church—the anger is snuffed out. You could say that you are sublimating your anger into productive work, or you have better things to do with your time. People fuss and fume over their settlements or their custody arrangements. If your attorney thinks it is fair, put it out of your mind. When you try to "get back" at someone, you lock yourself into a never-ending round of grief. If you really feel like you must do something because your rights were trampled on, do it through your attorney.

Anger, as flamboyant as it is sometimes, can also be quite subtle. It has a lot to do with expectations. We can set ourselves up for an angry moment. A small child is going to feel different before going off to visit a parent than he/she does when returning from the visit. You have to know these situations and not have unrealistic expectations about them. If you know that your child or stepchild always comes home a little moody from visits to his/her mother, don't be expecting the child to come home differently this time. Such unrealistic expectation sets you up for disappointment, and maybe even some anger toward the child or the child's mother.

Our twenty-two year old son was spending some time with us while going to the community college. My wife walked by his room. She paused and said, "I thought he was going to keep his room neater." I responded, "He hasn't kept his room neat for twenty-two years, why did you think that he was going to keep it neat today." Be realistic. Don't just wish, and then be angry when your wish doesn't come true.

Anger usually starts in the head—with our thoughts, our plans, our expectations. When we do not receive the expected response, we get angry. We decide something unjust is going on. The anger moves from our head to our hands, so to speak. We want "revenge" for things not going as we thought they should. This is where self-control comes in. Even though we feel angry, we do not have to express it. In fact, anger can even be avoided if we see it coming. The more you are aware of yourself, especially your thoughts and feelings, the more warning you will have that anger is coming.

What do you do to avoid anger? Take a hike if you have to. Go to the store till you cool off. Go to church, to a movie, to the shopping mall. Anything is better than having a fit of anger. You will be surprised how

quickly it passes if you change the environment. Tell
your partner what you are doing. "I'm going to the
store till I cool down."

I don't know where people ever got the idea that
the only way to get rid of anger is to express it. After
you express it, you are left with guilt over all the
dumb, exaggerated things you said. Better to get rid
of anger by rethinking the situation and realizing that
perhaps what you had expected was a little too much,
possibly even unrealistic, or maybe that's just the way
certain people are and you need to accept them as
they are.

A child's anger can come from many places. The
child may be angry because he or she feels helpless
to do anything about the environment that means so
much to him/her. His/her whole world has changed,
and the child has not only had nothing to do with it,
but also nothing to say about it. When you lose control and negative things happen to you, anger is a
normal reaction. When the father and mother you
love no longer love each other, you lose your happy
home. This is a tough situation to be in.

Most of a child's pleas or complaints are met with
the attitude that children do not understand adult
problems. This is not necessarily coming from in-
sensitivity—it is partly true, and partly an attempt
on the parents' part to cope. You cannot give the child
what he or she desires—the former marriage. But
you need to understand that the child's anger is not
unjustified. Anger comes in all sizes, at all ages, and

it holds a destructive power over those who succumb to it.

One child could not tolerate correction from either of his biological parents or his new stepparent. Whenever a parent tried to correct him, he would explode in anger. But at school he was a model student, taking correction in stride. Even at his young age, he felt he had a social image at school that he needed to uphold. Another child expressed a passive anger that looked like coping from the outside. For quite some time, no one noticed that she was withdrawing, and spending more and more time alone in her room. Neither of these children's reaction to anger was the parent's fault. We all know that sometimes even the best of parents are the last to know what is going with their children. Sometimes it even takes a loud announcement from outside the home to clue us in on problems.

A group of teenage boys bravely approached a mother and told her that they thought her son was severely depressed. They saw major changes in him. She had seen only minor changes, but his friends' visit spurred her to action. After talking to her son, she realized that his friends were right. She followed their advice and got help for her son.

A child's anger can come from stress, and stress comes from change. Be slow to change too much too soon in a youngster's life. Maybe a new home can be helpful in some ways, but new people in the house, new living arrangements, and maybe a new school are enough changes for six months. Depending upon the child's personality, reactions will be different. Children need structure. A remarriage disrupts their need for structure, and may cause angry outbursts or passive withdrawal. As soon as possible, provide them a structure that will help them to feel secure. Give them their own place to eat, to sleep, and to study. Without being rigid, have set times for meals, for sleep, and for homework. Getting into a routine can help both you and your children.

You may often feel like your child's whipping post. How are you supposed to handle all this anger? Taking that anger and trying to take the edge off it, so that the family can blend, is a part of what you are called to do. The parent in the blended family, in many respects, is like the parent of a child with ADD: you have to constantly work with the child. You feel like you are gaining ground, and suddenly you're back to square one. Sometimes the child hates you. Tension mounts. Tears flow. The doctor is called. The medication is changed. Things settle down. Then you say something simple, like, "Pick up your shirt," and the child goes into an unannounced eruption of physical and verbal abuse. And this continues, on and off, perhaps for the rest of your life. Sometimes you can calm them down; sometimes you can only endure it. If you persevere, the child's eventual maturity and self-awareness will lessen the anger.

The battle over a child's anger is never clearly defined. You can never pick the day on which you've won the battle. Things gradually seem to be more tolerable. Anger recedes slowly, like the tide. Suddenly it is low tide. One day most of the anger is gone. This does not mean all the problems are gone, but it does mean that the rough edge of anger does not have to be dealt with constantly.

No matter how frustrated you may get at times, remember that you are only one of many parents that are struggling with children who have special needs. You are trying to blend a family. And you have God's help, whether you always realize it or not. You have a vocation, a call from God, to help this family blend.

CHAPTER SEVEN

Loss and Its Effects on Us

There is one thing that everyone in the blended family shares: They have each suffered a loss. Whether through death or divorce, everyone has lost a spouse, a parent, or a child. This is good to remember. It is easy to remember our own losses, of course, but we sometimes forget that those around us have suffered losses too. In a blended family, this should never be forgotten.

Loss does funny things to us. It can make us pity ourselves. You don't want that attitude running through a whole family. It can make us feel guilty, with thoughts of "I should have" or "I shouldn't have." Guilt often leads to resentment, which makes us want to strike back and get even for our pain.

If you feel any of these emotions, dump them. You have a new job now. You are the head of a blended family. If you feel sorry for yourself, you will be consumed with the past. The job lies ahead. Do not consume yourself with something you did or with something someone else did.

Some biological parents find they cannot accept the fact that their children are living with a stepparent. One biological father became so angry every time he thought about this that he had a hard time relating to his stepchildren. His mind was always on his biological children. He was so torn up by the guilt he felt for leaving his children that he could not accept himself, and so he could not accept his stepchildren. It was only after he faced up to his guilt that his anger subsided. Guilt compounds problems. We can cut our emotional problems easily in half by getting rid of guilt.

Guilt adds an extra burden to any problem we have. It drags our spirits down. If you are truly guilty, confess it. Put it in God's hands. That should be the end of guilt. Guilt keeps us from loving one another and coming up with creative solutions to problems. Once you get the guilt out of the way, you can deal with your former spouse much better, especially in terms of the children. One woman told her counselor that she hates to see her former husband when she takes the kids there for a visit. "He and his wife are cordial, and so am I," she says. "I do this for Amy, my daughter. But the visit reminds me of all the things I did that I am ashamed of, and it reminds me of all the things he did to me for so many years. I will feel a lot better when I get these things resolved."

Loss can also make us bitter, leading us to distrust. A blended family needs none of this. Loss can leave you feeling flat. Certainly remarriage and love does away with a lot of that, but a little bit of leftover bitterness can come out in subtle ways—in short remarks, sarcasm, and things better left unsaid. It is dangerous to leave bitterness hanging around. An analogy might be leaving a can of uncovered gasoline in your utility room. It is safe, as long as the vapors don't build up and the pilot light in the furnace doesn't catch hold of them. Unresolved bitterness can hurt you gradually over a period of time, or it can hurt you quickly with a sudden flare up.

You need to work on your feelings of loss so that you can relate to your former spouse. It is so hard for us to put down our old hatreds. As much as we may deny it, hatred gives us some sense of pleasure. It might even evoke a feeling of power over another. To put hate aside seems weak, an admission of loss. It isn't. Dropping hatred, even if you need the help of a counselor to get rid of, it is a gift to yourself. Remember, Jesus told us that even if we were offering a gift at the altar, if we have hatred in our hearts, we must leave the gift and reconcile with our brother or sister first. Of course, you cannot reconcile with someone if that would be putting yourself back into the situation where you originally got hurt. But you do have to try to change your heart, so that you no longer feel resentment from your loss, but the peace that comes from forgiving it. I remember

Father Bernard Häring, the great moral theologian, saying that even if you can't love your enemies, as the gospel says, you can at least pray for them. Then loss will not leave you with negative feelings.

Some of us do not put thoughts aside very easily, and I do not mean to imply that "dumping thoughts" is as simple as making the intention, but some of us are more obsessive than others. I knew a man who was so consumed with thoughts of his divorce that he could not even sleep. His work was impaired. He could not put the thoughts down. He needed professional help. My job was to convince him that there was no shame in that. This man emotionally wrestled with the idea of seeking professional help, thinking it would be a sign that he was weak or defective. I tried to point out that some people just don't have the ability to forget as easily as others because our minds are different. Some minds can do math, for example, while others write poetry. In the same way, some people are naturally patient, while others are not.

Eventually, the man went to see a doctor. A prescription medication not only helped him sleep, it also helped his mind stop running away with thoughts about the divorce. I explained to him that if he were diabetic, he would not feel bad about taking insulin. "Insulin helps your body handle sugar," I told him. "This pill helps your body handle thoughts you don't want any longer."

I'm not pushing medication, but I do know that

the ending of a relationship, even if it is for the best, is one of the toughest human situations to handle. And if you are getting into a blended family, you do not need any extra baggage to carry around. You need a clear mind and a peaceful spirit. For some, today's antidepressants from the hands of a good doctor can do wonders. When you have prayed for weeks for peace of mind, and then your doctor offers you an antidepressant, don't you think that this might be a modern-day answer to your prayers?

The Effects of Loss on Our Children

Sometimes we do not realize the depth of the loss that our children face, nor do we realize the number of losses a child faces when a family goes through a divorce. In Laura Walters book, *There's a New Family in my House,* she tells the story of a ten-year-old boy named Allan. This story is often typical. After Allan's mother and father divorce, he stays with his mother and experiences his first loss: his father's leave-taking. So Allan bonds more closely with his mother, the custodial parent. But he loses that exclusive relationship with her when she remarries. Eventually, he bonds with his stepfather fairly well. But then his mother has a new baby, with his stepfather, and everyone's attention is diverted from Allan to the new baby. He loses his third relationship, with his stepfather.

Allen tries to get back into the family circle by doing what he knows how to do—tease his new little sister. For this, his mother and stepfather punish him.

Now Allan misses his father, and he asks to go live with the biological dad, who is still single. After a while, the mother sends him to his father, and they bond. But then the father remarries. Allan loses his fourth exclusive relationship. He bonds with his new stepmother, and then a new baby comes along. His fifth attempt at intimacy fails.

Allan is depressed. No wonder. The little guy has tried and tried, and always ends up on the outside— or at least what he considers to be the outside. This is no fault of his parents, and certainly no fault of Allan's. But it is a common scenario. You need to take special care to make sure that you attend to losses your children feel as their lives change.

Besides family losses, there are other very real losses in the child's life that you might ignore or be unaware of. Changing schools was always a trauma for me when my family moved. Leaving old friends and making new ones is not always easy. In the former school, I had certain things established. I was on the basketball team, for example. In the new school, I had to prove myself all over again, as a good basketball player, to people who did not even know me. In some cases, in fact, the new school didn't even have a basketball team.

All these little losses go on behind the scenes, so to speak. Adults might not even notice them, but they hurt children. When they happen along with the loss of a parent, and the gaining of a stepparent, it can be a heavy burden for a child to carry around.

Falling in love is an absorbing experience, and having a new baby is an engrossing event, but it is specifically during times like these that you need to take special care your children do not feel left out. Try to make sure the children know that none of the "left out" feelings they have are their fault. Allan, in our story above, needed to be reassured that, even though he made five attempts to bond and felt like he failed each time, it had nothing to do with him. He was loved and loveable.

Walters suggests that you try to do the things the child likes. If the child likes bedtime reading, make sure you do that for him or her. Also make yourself available to the child. Have time just for him or her. You may also help the children discover their special talents or interests, and once they have, encourage them to work at these. If a new school does not have activities that the children are interested in, help them find an organization that does: church youth groups, YM/WCA, or Boys and Girls Clubs. As a child feels more important as an individual, he or she begins to feel like he/she has something to contribute to the family. The feeling of loss and isolation is minimized.

Again, the best thing that you can do for a child in a blended family is to have a civil relationship with the absent biological parent. When you get along with your former spouse, it makes the child feel like things are all right in his/her new environment. The loss is mitigated. When you cooperate with your former spouse, it does even more to help your child deal with his/her sense of loss. A healthy relationship with your former spouse makes loss less stinging. If you are not on good terms with your former spouse, you can at least make sure that things do not get any worse. Don't say anything negative about your ex in front of the child. And refrain from asking the child questions about his/her biological parent. Questions imply investigation, and that automatically makes a child think that something is wrong.

Loss will negatively affect everyone in a blended family, some more than others. But the loss can also be the driving force that unites the family. That's what families are for—to give everyone a place to belong— and the mature person knows that children do not exist to fulfill their parents. It is the parent's job to look after the children. If everyone looks out for one another, and no one is made to feel left out, the sting of loss can be greatly minimized.

CHAPTER EIGHT

The Extended Family

The boundaries of the blended family are stretched considerably when the extended family is included. One middle-school girl told her teacher that she had sixteen grandparents. The teacher looked at her sideways and said that was impossible. But the girl went on to explain that she had two biological parents and two stepparents. Her four parents each had four living parents. Four times four makes sixteen grandparents.

When you get into a blended family, relationships add up. This can cause confusion. We may have a tendency to "rank" grandparents, or to like some and dislike others. Bringing all the grandparents into the family circle may be difficult at times, but in the long run, it is worth it for everybody. Mary Ann Wolinski, in *A Heart of Wisdom: Marital Counseling With Older and Elderly Couples* (Brunner-Routledge, 1990), has some interesting ideas about grandparents in blended families. I have taken the liberty of expanding on some of them.

Sometimes, allowing the grandparents into the home brings with it a lot of ghosts of bygone years. Especially former in-laws recall relationships of the past. This will not always be comfortable. "Having my ex-husband's mother and father over to the house for a graduation party was not easy," one woman recalls. "It reminded me of all the difficult times we had during the separation and divorce. They made things very difficult for me. They never formally apologized, but they did mellow with time." Having them around reminded the woman of the hard times, but it was good for her in the sense that it helped her realize she could finally deal with those feelings. The past was no longer so frightening.

An extra benefit of having grandparents around is that the children love it. It gives them a good feeling. But a common problem is that the grandparents are not as sensitive to all the subtleties in the extended family. They may offend one of the parents, and perhaps not be invited back to a family gathering. One grandmother, on a visit to her son's blended family, created quite a stir. She came storming out of the bedroom. "Those children (meaning the stepchildren) don't even know the Hail Mary. What kind of religious training are you giving them?" She was addressing her son, but the message was meant for his new wife. After a few experiences like this, the wife was not eager to have her mother in-law visit again.

In such situations, a good deal of communication has to go on if Grandma is going to stay in the loop. The son has to talk to his wife, and he also has to talk to his mother about his wife's feelings and the priority of the marital relationship. The beginning of a marriage is the toughest time for learning how to get along with in-laws. In this story, as in most, things mellowed with time.

One of the difficulties that some people run into with grandparents is a difference in attitudes and beliefs. The grandparents might not see remarriage as positively as we see it here. Some see a second marriage as not quite as good as the first marriage, especially if the first marriage ended in divorce. This stems from the times they grew up in, and the ways they were taught. It may reflect, to some extent, their inability to change their thinking. Try to keep in mind that their lack of tolerance is not your fault, and you still might be able to enjoy their company. There are positive reasons for fostering a relationship between the grandparents and the children.

It is good for us to remember that grandparents are often the forgotten ones. Grandparents had nothing to do with the divorce, and they had nothing to say about the arrangements. Frequently, one grandparent or another is left suffering because an in-law is mad at his or her former spouse. I have seen many grandparents who were completely shut out of their grandchild's life by an angry ex-spouse.

It is a real heartbreaker to see this. Grandparents

are left wondering what their grandchildren are like, perhaps even what they look like. They wonder whether or what the grandchildren think about them. If the grandparent is not a bad influence on the child, the two should not be deprived of one another's company.

Walters suggests that, especially in the first year of marriage, parents should instruct grandparents in how to deal with their children. This makes sense. Many grandparents have never dealt with stepchildren. They might appreciate advice. For example, it might not be obvious to them that they are "favoring" their biological heirs over their step-grandchildren, or, conversely, that in trying so hard to not play favorites they are actually slighting the biological ones.

The greatest reason for having grandparents around is for what it does for them and the children. It gives grandparents a feeling of continuity in their lives, and actually helps them to deal with feelings about death and mortality. Seeing our children's children has always been considered a great blessing, going back to biblical times. In a very real way, grandparents have passed on life as God intended, and it is a gift to be able to enjoy that. It is also helpful for the children, who get to see a little bit of living family history. Knowing where you came from helps you to know yourself better. Knowing where your stepparents came from helps you to understand them better. It might not all make sense right now, for the children, but as they get older, the memories might help them to better understand family life, and themselves. I see traits in my sons that I saw in my own father. I see traits in my wife that I can see in her parents. Grandparents help us to see the "big picture" of our lives, and that makes everything more understandable.

But beyond such genealogical considerations, the value of grandparents is severely underestimated. They provide a great contribution to the family in terms of wisdom. I hear my father-in-law giving my sons his philosophy on money. He not only tells them prudent ways to use it and invest it, but he also tells them to keep money in its proper perspective and never let it become too important. Little things like that are important in the long run. We may not always think of what they tell us as wisdom, but they have the distinct advantage of having seen more of life than we have. They have seen how things turn out after certain choices are made.

Even their financial contributions are sometimes overlooked. Grandparents have made life easier for many families. This generation of young adults is in the position to inherit more wealth than any generation before it. This is due to the elder generation, those who are in the role of grandparents. Will you have the wisdom to use that wealth wisely? This can have great social and spiritual ramifications. Perhaps you should listen carefully to the wisdom in your family.

Grandparents will always mean different things to

different people. To some people they may always be the in-laws, but to some they are Mom and Dad, and to some they are Grandma and Grandpa. They will have their ups and downs, like everyone else. But try to remember there is a lot more going on here than just what meets your eye. If they grate on one person's nerves, they may soothe another's. The rule in the blended family, regardless of how many grandparents there are, is to be kind to all of them and give each of them the benefit of the doubt.

A very good virtue for the blended family to cultivate is hospitality. A Christian family should receive every guest as Christ. That was Saint Benedict's motto in his monasteries and Mother Teresa's motto on the streets of the ghetto. Rather than fighting for privacy, loosen up. Let all the grandparents, and everyone else connected with your children's lives—aunts and uncles, cousins, etc.—have access to your home.

Chapter Nine

A Success Story

*M*eredith grew up in a small town in a typical Catholic family. She had two older sisters and attended Catholic school. Her mother and father loved them all. But Meredith's mother died when she was quite young. Some time later her father remarried.

Meredith's sisters did not receive their new stepmother very well. They acted independently, as if they did not need her. Meredith, on the other hand, was more dependent on her stepmother. She allowed the stepmother to take care of her, and to tuck her in bed at night. But her stepmother never tucked Meredith's sisters into bed.

Meredith remembers growing up in that blended family, and she resolves today, now that she is the mother of a blended family, not to make the same mistakes. "My stepmother should have seen through my sisters' defenses. She should have known, even *though they acted as if they did not need her, that they still needed her."*

Meredith goes on to say, *"My stepmother was a good woman, but she should have tried harder to relate to my sisters. I just don't think that my father and stepmother were involved enough with us as children."*

Meredith met a nice divorced man, with a teenage daughter, and they married. Anxious to avoid her stepmother's mistakes of not getting involved, Meredith was determined to be a real part of the blended family. She set out to make friends with her husband's daughter.

"I know she already had a mother that she was living with. She did not need another mother, but I was determined that, at least, I was going to be her friend and a role model. I would not be able to stand it if my stepdaughter did not like me, or if she avoided her father because she did not want to be around me."

Meredith was certainly motivated to make this blended family work, but the true benefit came one day when Meredith and her husband went to pick up his daughter for a visit. Meredith remained in the car while her husband went into the home of his ex-wife. A few minutes after he went into the house, his ex-wife came out to the car and said to Meredith, *"Please come in. I want you to know that you are always welcome in my home."*

"That was the beginning of a wonderful relation-

ship," Meredith said. "Since then, she has always let me have a free and open relationship with my stepdaughter, and she has never interfered or been jealous. In fact, we get along so well with my husband's former wife that we have mutual friends, and it isn't unusual for us to find ourselves out at dinner with them and another couple."

Whenever there is a family social event, Meredith and her husband are invited to the home. Meredith and the biological mother both attended the girl's softball games and other activities. The girl is naturally closer to her biological mother, but she has a good relationship with her stepmother. She will sometimes come to Meredith with a problem and ask, "How would you run this by my mother if you were me?" This always makes Meredith feel good.

Because of the good relationship she has with her stepdaughter, Meredith is able to be a help to the whole family. When her husband, the biological father, wanted to see his daughter more, he found she was always "busy." Meredith helped him understand that the young lady was at that age where friends are very important and relations outside the home are being seriously forged. She helped her husband settle on more "adult time" with his daughter, like meeting her for lunch.

Meredith stayed involved with her stepdaughter, but she knew when to stay out of the way. "If my husband and his ex-wife were trying to solve a problem with my stepdaughter, I stayed out of it," she said.

"They were the parents, and they were perfectly capable of handling it. I also made it a point to never get into any arguments with my stepdaughter. She was not living with me, and she was not my primary responsibility at the time. I did the same thing with my feelings. I never complained to my husband about his daughter. Not that there was much to complain about, but there were times when I could have. I am so glad I kept silent." Meredith told me that she disliked anger. She thought it would be a real shame for a child to have to live in a situation where anger was always present, so if she had to bite her tongue once in a while, she did so. She never regretted doing this.

Meredith followed the same philosophy with her husband. If her husband and his ex-wife had a problem to deal with, like who should pay a particular bill, she stayed out of it. In fact she did not even want to know about it because, once again, they were *"perfectly capable"* of handling the problem.

Meredith has a willingness to get involved, and also a willingness to stay out of things when her involvement is not necessary. This has saved her a great deal of psychic energy. Meredith's ability to handle her neutral position has been so successful that sometimes her husband or her husband's ex-wife will ask her to talk to their daughter.

Meredith and her husband have two boys. The stepdaughter, who frequently visits, has become a good friend to the boys.

When you look at this successful blended family, you realize that it has added great joy to both families. It gave Meredith a stepdaughter. She says that this is probably the only daughter she will have. The stepdaughter and former spouse both gained a friend in Meredith.

The success of this blended family did not happen by accident. Everyone started out with a certain amount of good will, a lack of hostility, and a desire to cooperate. Meredith tried to make friends with her stepdaughter, and the girl allowed Meredith to be her friend. The ex-wife reached out to Meredith and allowed her to have a free and open relationship with her daughter. Everyone worked together to make this blended family a success, and their efforts paid off. They have a peaceful and loving family.

Perhaps some people will think that Meredith should have spoken up more. Some might believe she should have involved herself in her husband's affairs, and she should have criticized her stepdaughter on occasion. I don't think so. We do not communicate just to communicate. There is such a thing as too much communication. There is no need to tell people things that are petty and that they do not need to hear. Unless her husband was terribly distressed by his problems, I don't think Meredith needed to get involved. Unless the stepdaughter was doing something that was dangerous to herself or others, I don't think she had to tell her husband every feeling she had. Discretion is a sign of maturity. When to speak up and when to hold back is always a tough choice. We need to pray for the wisdom to say what helps and refrain from speaking of things that are hurtful for no reason.

I tell this story to show what is possible. Amazing things happen when reasonable people love one another. Everyone may not be able to reach this ideal, but perhaps you can make efforts that will improve relationships in your blended family. One of the things that Meredith often says is that when you marry a divorced person you also marry part of their past. In other words, you have to be willing to deal with their children from the first marriage and try to blend them into a relationship with your own children. You have to be willing to develop a relationship with your spouse's ex-spouse. You have to do what you can to make the relationship positive and cooperative, for the sake of the children and for the sake of your marriage. That's vocation.

CHAPTER TEN

The Non-custodial Parent

T he non-custodial parent is often in a helpless situation. First of all, he or she has to deal with not being around the children everyday. He/she may have taken the family for granted up until now, but with the realization of loss comes grief. The whole atmosphere, from the non-custodial parent's point of view, hinges on the custodial parent's attitude. But the non-custodial parent has to be cooperative. Some parents find it hard enough being separated from their children, but when they are still struggling with their ex-spouse, the whole situation can really become unbearable. Part of the responsibility of the parent in a blended family is to be just. As Pope Paul VI said so succinctly, "If you want peace work for justice."

You cannot expect peace in your family if you, as the custodial parent, continue to use custody for leverage in a relationship. The same holds true for the non-custodial parent. Rules are rules. As unjust as you feel they may be, you have to abide by them until they are changed. Fudging on what time you return the children to their custodial parent, or not keeping visitation appointments, is hurtful, especially to the children. When the custodial parent changes visitation dates or fails to have the child ready for a visit, this also is unfair. Every effort needs to be made, both by biological parents and stepparents, to be just to one another.

After his divorce, Tom spent a long time grieving over the loss of his child. He saw the boy weekly, but he thought he was not having the kind of influence on his son that he would have if he saw the boy everyday. To make matters worse, his ex-wife and he did not communicate well. Sometimes, Tom would come to pick the child up and she would say, "I thought it was tomorrow." She would often tell him that he had to have his son home early because they were going to dinner with the in-laws, or doing something else that she had obviously planned to cut into his prescribed time with the boy.

Tom's grief lessened when he married a woman who had two children of her own. He knew his responsibility was to be a good stepfather, so he did the best he could to bond with his wife's children, but it was tough going at first. In some ways the children accepted him, but in other ways they did not.

Tom decided he was doing a poor job as a stepfather and a mediocre job as a biological father. He felt trapped, but he kept on trying. Much of what he was feeling was his own negative perception of himself as a father.

Then Tom and his wife had a child of their own. This was a happy time for them. Tom wanted to make sure he did the best job he could with this child. When his son from the first marriage came to visit, Tom tried to help him bond with his new little brother, and, of course, with the stepchildren. Tom always greeted his first son warmly, and made sure he had plenty of time for the boy. He reserved time to talk to his son alone, in case the boy wanted to tell him something in private, but he also included his stepchildren in any outings that were planned during the visit. He felt that this was the only fair and just way to do it.

Some well-meaning friends chided him. "That isn't fair to your own child. You are taking your time and attention away from him." But Tom was firm on this point. He did not believe that including his stepchildren or his new baby was a slight to his first son. He wanted his first son see them all, collectively, as family. "I think it would have looked more artificial if I'd left everybody else at home and went out with my son. It would give a confused message to my son, and make my stepchildren feel different or left out."

Usually, the things that Tom does together with his son and stepchildren are not of the big amusement park or shopping binge ilk, but he tries to have *an "average" day with them. They might go to the hardware store, swim in the pool, and go to church. Tom cooks out, or makes breakfast after Mass. "I want to have a normal relationship with my child when he comes to visit," he says.*

Tom tries hard. But he still has regrets about the way he acted during and after the divorce. "Life would be a lot more simple if my ex-wife and I had acted more maturely," he says. "I wish we could start all over, and not say the things we said. My advice to anyone going through a divorce is to bite your tongue and compromise. It is faster, cheaper in terms of legal fees, and you will not have all those hard feelings getting the way of your relationship with the kids."

Sometimes Tom thinks it is too late to make a good working relationship with his ex-wife, but he is trying now for the sake of his son. Things have changed very little, but he says that he tries to keep hope alive. He knows it would be easy to throw in the towel and avoid the conflict, but he plods ahead. He wants a relationship with his son.

Tom's wife gives him encouragement. She tells him what a good father he is, and that someday all the children will recognize the efforts he made to be with them. This helps Tom. He says that Mother Teresa's words—that God calls us to be faithful, not successful—are words he tries to live by.

There are many fathers and mothers in situations like Tom's. It is a tough road to hoe, when you have to battle to get through to your children. Yet, you have to keep trying and you have to keep your hope alive. If you remain patient and do not escalate the hostilities, you always have the hope that things can get better. In the meantime, enjoy whatever time you can have with your children. Do not miss out on quality time because you are angry.

The Single Non-custodial Parent

Not all non-custodial parents remarry, of course. Divorced single parents have to figure out how to fit into the blended family their ex-spouse has made. If they are mature, they can be a great help to the blended family.

Jack lives alone. His ex-wife has custody of the children. He works, goes to the gym, and goes to bed early. He reads a lot. On the whole, his life is routine and boring. He is learning how to cope with it. It is a big change for him, after life with two children around the house. He really does not like to be alone, but he does not want to rush into a relationship just so he will not be alone. When it is his day with the children, he is punctual.

When Jack picks the kids up, everything at his ex-wife's house seems lively. She's had a child with her second husband, and they also have his children from his first marriage. Jack's two children are very happy there. Friends constantly surround them. Jack feels almost inadequate taking them to his lonely apartment, which is rather quiet, and he is afraid that it is a bit dull for the kids compared to where they live now.

Jack sees his ex-wife's new husband. He is sociable. He offers Jack coffee. Jack declines, not sure what to do. The whole place seems nice, much nicer than his place. He has to remind himself that the children are coming to see him, not his home. He takes the children home, and he makes breakfast. They talk, go for a walk, and stop in the playground. They play with some of their former friends in the neighborhood. They seem to be having a good time. Jack is satisfied.

He makes lunch. They go to a bookstore. Jack loves to read and he has been trying to pass on the love of books to the children. They resist. They rent a video, order a pizza. The next morning they go to Mass, and out to breakfast. Boring?

"This is my life," Jack says. "If I lived on a farm in Dakota they would have to adapt to my lifestyle there. It just so happens I'm a single guy in the same city, so they adapt to my lifestyle here." Jack is amazed how the children adapt. They like being with him, not for what he has, but for who he is.

Jack still does not know how to relate to his ex-wife's family. He feels like the odd man out. He tries to be polite and gracious because he knows that this is the home of his ex-wife and of his children. Every time he shows respect in that home, he is helping his children feel comfortable. He makes every effort to be as sociable as possible, for the children's sake.

Jack is aware that his children like it when he talks to their stepfather about mutual friends or similarities in their work. The children feel like there is a connection between the two households. Jack goes out of his way to promote this connection, because his main goal in life is the children.

Jack has learned to enjoy as much as he can about being alone. He uses his free time as judiciously as he can, and he tries to develop hobbies to keep himself busy. But he always is careful that he does not get too involved with hobbies, so he can be available to the children whenever they need him.

Jack has made some serious attempts to make himself more content in his altered lifestyle. Simply by being there, as a well-balanced and mature father, Jack has given the children the opportunity to see their father on a regular basis and have a consistent relationship with him. His ex-wife has been cooperative and appreciative of Jack. In all this, Jack has made himself a better father to his children and a support to his ex-wife's blended family. They count on him.

Sometimes they count on his to do the unexpected. When his ex-wife and her husband were called out of town on an emergency, they dropped all the children off at Jack's house. They consider him extended family—someone who will be there for them and be willing to take the children. Jack is happy to have the children, and happy to help.

Jack could have easily been a disgruntled bachelor. He could have been jealous of his ex-wife's more affluent lifestyle, and he could have taken out his anger on his wife. He could have acted immaturely, forgetting to show up for visits with the children or bringing the children home late, just to cause annoyance. Because he chose to be mature, he has been a big help to the extended family, and his children have a healthy relationship with their father.

Consistency is vital for non-custodial parents. Non-custodial parents need to be counted on to make regular contact with their children, even in long-distance relationships. The farther away a parent lives from his or her child, the more important it is to have a cooperative relationship with his/her ex-spouse. Parents have to realize that it is good for their children to have a consistent relationship with both of them, and even that the children's relationship with their stepparents is helped when both parents remain a vital part of their lives.

In *Making Peace in Your Stepfamily: Surviving and Thriving as Parents and Stepparents* (Hyperion Press, 1993), Harald H. Bloomfield and Robert B. Korey make some suggestions for non-custodial parents and their children who are a great distance apart. They suggest that you call often. Write frequently, and enclose a self-addressed stamped envelope so that the child can easily reply to your letter. Audiocassettes are another means of communication. They also suggest that the absent parent and his or her child watch the same TV programs, go to the same movies, and follow the same sports teams, so that they have more to share.

The key for the non-custodial parent is to try to get along with the whole blended family. The more people you can get along with in this new family arrangement, the better it will be for you and your children. One of the positive things that can come out of a blended family is that children develop a great ability to cope. If you want that to happen, you have to be a model. If you want peace, work for justice. It benefits everyone.

CHAPTER ELEVEN

The Tone of the Family

Michael was biological father to a ten-year-old son and stepfather to a twelve-year-old daughter. He was one of those fathers that constantly evaluated his work. One day when his wife was not at home, his stepdaughter asked to go to a movie with some boys and girls in her class. This was the first time he remembered her going out with girls *and* boys, so he was not sure what to do. He knew most of the kids, and the parents who were driving, so he agreed to let her go.

While she was gone, Michael was distracted. He wondered whether this was what his wife would have done. He was distracted in relating to his son, who stayed home. Three hours later, when the stepdaughter did not come home, he started to worry even more. He thought that maybe he should not have permitted her to go. He thought, "I should have left this decision to my wife, at least the first time." Finally, one of the parents drove up with a car full of laughing kids.

"They talked me into taking them out for pizza," the laughing parent said.

"Great, great," Michael replied, trying to act like he did not have a care in the world.

Many parents and stepparents labor over whether they make the right decisions. Even more worry about whether they are doing a good job as parents. Michael probably worried more than most, but he managed to break out of this worry mold one day when, in confession, he told the priest how much he obsessed about being a good father and stepfather.

"Do you love your children and stepchildren?" the priest asked.

"Of course," said Michael. "More than anything in the world."

"Then," said the priest, "you are doing a good job."

The priest went on, "You judge the quality of your parenting by the tone of your parenting, the overall, general attitude that you have toward your vocation. If you love them and you try to show it, the tone of your parenting is good. Therefore the job you are doing is good."

Michael walked out of there with an entirely new feeling about himself and his vocation as a parent and stepparent. No longer did he pick at every little thing he did. He just trusted that he was doing a good job in God's eyes because he loved and he tried to show that love.

The blended family is not about sentimental love, but it is about all the work and effort that love implies. It is about the kind of love that is patient and kind. It is about the kind of love that makes you available when you want to do something else. It is about the kind of love that makes you persevere when you are rejected. This kind of love makes the family blend together, and that is a part of your vocation. It is the law that Jesus himself gave us. "Love one another."

We might not think that love is a very appropriate measure of how well a person has done a job. We usually measure how well a person has done by the results: how much has been accomplished and the quality of those accomplishments. But when you judge how well you have done as a parent in a family, you need to see the entire picture—from the time your first child was born or you first met your stepchildren, until the time that the last child leaves home. Take this whole picture, from beginning to end, and judge it in terms of whether you loved and tried to show love. You cannot judge yourself by any other standard, especially not by specific instances. You cannot say, "If I had not let the kids go to that party, they never would have gotten into drinking." You cannot say, "I was too easy on Johnny when he was in the second grade, and therefore we had a hard time with him for a couple of years." You cannot judge the quality of your parenting based on a few specific scenes from the past.

You should never go back over your life and feel

guilty about your job as a parent because of what you have done at specific moments with the children. We all have had times when we put more of ourselves into a job than we should have and neglected the children. We all have had times when we thought that making money, or obtaining a particular possession, or even our involvement in some worthwhile project, was more important than time with the children. As time goes by, we see how foolish our judgment was. But mistakes and bad judgments are part of life. Don't judge yourself on these.

You can only judge what kind of parent you have been by the overall tone of your parenting. Overall, what kind of parent were you? Overall, were you trying? Did you try to show love to your children? Did you try to do the best thing for your children? That's why I say that the most important thing is love. Love creates the tone. Trying to show love creates the tone. So we need to judge ourselves by the tone we created or tried to create in the family.

Some parents and stepparents unjustifiably feel like failures. They pour out stories of what a miserable job they did, of how they should have spent more time with their children or how they should have been firmer. As they berate themselves, I can see what a wonderful job they generally have done. They are looking at minute details, or solely at the results, but their whole tone had been a sincere effort to reach their children over a period of sixteen or seventeen years. They had made many sacrifices, involved themselves in the children's lives, endured put-downs and failures, and never gave up. They kept trying.

Catherine was married to a man with two daughters. He did not have custody of the children, but they visited for a month in the summer and every other weekend. Catherine had one daughter who was two years older than her husband's children.

Catherine had left her first marriage because of spousal abuse. The daughter was unaware of the abuse, and blamed her mother for leaving her father. Catherine's daughter was difficult to control. She skipped school, dabbled in drugs, and, in Catherine's words, "hung around with scary people." Catherine's husband supported her, but he could not do much with the girl, who kept reminding him that he was not her father.

Catherine never stopped trying and praying. She took her daughter to a counselor. When that did not work, she took the girl to a psychiatrist. The psychiatrist prescribed medication, which helped, but Catherine's daughter stopped taking the medication. Catherine left work so often for teacher conferences that her supervisor warned her about taking too much time off. She tried to get her daughter into a private girls' school, but she could not afford it.

Things grew worse. When her husband's daughters came to visit, he would not allow them to go out with his stepdaughter. It pained him and embarrassed Catherine, but there seemed to be nothing else to do.

"We can't trust my daughter," Catherine said. "I don't blame my husband for not letting his daughters go out with her."

Catherine's daughter eventually joined the Air Force. She had some problems there, but she did make it through. After her discharge, she seems to have settled down.

From my perspective, I see parents like Catherine and her husband as successful. The tone of their parenting over those sixteen or seventeen years was full of love. Why else would they try so hard? If they did not love, they could never have done the job they did for all those years. Even Catherine's husband, who could not get close to his stepdaughter, played a vital role of support, and his love kept him in a chaotic situation. I wish I could find the words to convey to them all the wonderful things that they have done. I wish that I could help them feel the satisfaction of a job well done, rather than think they have failed. They are successful parents and stepparents, whether they realize it or not, because the tone of their relationships over the years, with each other and with their children and stepchildren, has been one of love. Perhaps some day they will feel their well-deserved success.

Just because a child reaches adulthood restless and with a vague aim in life, does not mean that you have failed as parents or stepparents. The story is a long way from over, and you do not know what is going on in that child's mind. Maybe you will not even see the end of that story, but if the tone was the right tone, if love was the goal that pervaded most of your relationship with the child, you were a success. I would be willing to bet, based on what I have seen, that nine times out of ten, good results will show up eventually in that child's life. The uncertain or anguished child will eventually gain his or her bearings because he/she has been nurtured in a family where those bearings have been clear.

The tone is important because it is the only way we can judge a body of work that lasts for eighteen years or more. The only way we can judge the way we have performed our daily work, at which we earn a living, is by the tone. Whenever you do something for a long period of time, how else can you judge it? You can't judge it by isolated incidences. You can't judge it by the year you won an award. You have to judge it by the overall quality of the work, and that is the tone.

Parenting and stepparenting are no different. Since parenting is such a highly emotional vocation, you are tempted many times simply to make an emotional judgment of your work. When a child answers you back, you can feel crushed inside. You may act as a disciplinarian, but you still think, "What did I do to deserve that kind of treatment?" Sometimes you feel it is totally the child's fault. Other times you may examine yourself and think that you haven't given the child the time and attention he or she needs. It is good to take a quick look and examine yourself, but to dwell on what you did, to purposefully look for something that you did wrong, is unfair. This is especially true for parents in a blended family. A blended family is an extremely busy place, and you may find many unjustifiable reasons to blame yourself for something that goes wrong in the family. You might have given time to your stepchild, and now you think it was the biological child that needed your attention. You might have given your time to your spouse, and think you somehow neglected a child. You may have given your time to handling a situation with the in-laws, which left you no energy for the family. You can find a million things to blame yourself for. Resist the temptation. Look at the tone.

Adult children and stepchildren can also hurt you in a similar way if you are not aware of the tone of your relationship with them. If you don't hear from them or if they do not visit, it is not uncommon to say, "How come? Did I do something to deserve this? Have I been too clinging? Have I been too critical? Have I not allowed them to be themselves?" But do not dwell on such questions. Specific instances are not the important thing, even with adult children and stepchildren.

Do not play the blame game either. Just because "it" is not your fault, it does not have to be the adult child's fault. Sometimes things happen that are negative, and you have emotional reactions, but they may be no one's fault. Just because someone's feelings get hurt and they blame it on you, it does not mean that you were out to hurt their feelings; and just because your feelings get hurt, it does not mean that your adult children or stepchildren were out to hurt your feelings. Sometimes reality hurts feelings. Sometimes an adult child is just in a bad mood, and acts disrespectful. I don't mean that the child is not responsible for his or her behavior, but sometimes one's behavior is not intentional. Adult children can get busy with jobs and relationships and spend less time with you. If you have preconceived notions about how your relationship with your adult child or stepchild will be, you will inevitably be disappointed and end up pointing the finger of blame at someone. Their lives are time consuming. Reasons for hurt feelings may be nonexistent.

If you keep in mind that the most important thing you can do in the family is to keep loving one another, you will always be moving in the right direction. Days may come when you feel like you are moving in the exact opposite direction from where you should be going. At those times, you may not know how to handle your feelings. You might need some time out.

I had a friend who used to go to the office to work when he really became frustrated. "It was better than getting everyone else at home upset," he used to say. "At least at the office I got something positive done." He never felt bad when he did this. He never felt like he was not facing up to things. On the contrary, he believed he was facing the fact that, right at that time, he could not cope with things. If you don't have an office, you can go to church, the library, the bookstore, or your local 24-hour discount store. You will be surprised how a little change of venue can help you through a difficult time.

Keep in mind that it is the tone of your parenting that counts. This might pull you out of some bad moods when you think all is going haywire. It might help you when you are ready to blame yourself or others for the way things are going. Love sets the tone. Remember, it isn't just the feeling of love, but it is the hard-working love that let's everyone know you respect them and care about them.

CHAPTER TWELVE

Couple Conflict

D r. James H. Bray and John Kelly wrote a book called *Stepfamilies: Love, Marriage, and Parenting in the First Decade* (Broadway Books, 1999). The authors maintain that problems in the stepfamily often begin at the bottom and work their way up. In other words, the problems start with the children, and that creates problems in the couple relationship. Of course, this is not the only way a problem can start in stepfamily. A problem between the parent and stepparent can create a problem with the children. It isn't the only way to look at a problem, but it is an interesting way to look at a family problem. It is just one more point of view that might help. Later I am going to discuss inner peace, which is where it really all begins. But for now I find the more points of view you have about a family problem, the better chance you have of coming to a solution. Many points of view also keep you from being closed-minded. It is like walking around a house and seeing it from all sides instead from just the front.

Mark was the stepfather in a blended family. His wife had two children, a boy eight-years-old and a girl ten-years-old. Mark had one child of his own, who lived with his ex-wife. Since Mark's biological son lived out of town, he visited only on holidays and during the summer. Mark and his present wife, Linda, got along very well. One of the reasons for this was the age of the children. Children between the ages of eight and eleven are perhaps at their most placid stage of development. Home is still the number one place in their minds, and Mom and Dad are still the number one entertainment. Therefore, Bray and Kelly would most likely say that it was only natural that Mark and Linda were getting along so well. No problems were rising up from the children to the parents.

If you look at children at both ends of the spectrum, you would have to say that newborns, with all the attention they need, probably create more tension in the marital relationship than two children between eight and eleven. How would Mark and Linda be faring if they had a three-month-old child? That's probably not a fair question, but it is an important idea. When teens are displaying their wide range of emotions and you are battling their attempts to be too independent too early, the strain on the marriage is often overlooked. You should be aware of the strain. It may be that you should concentrate on paying more attention to your spouse. Remember, the marital relationship is always primary. If it takes a back seat to the parent-child relationship, the marriage fails.

But let's return to Mark and Linda and their two placid children. Everything was going along fine. They all had a good winter and a fine spring. And then came summer. Mark's son came to live with them for a month. He was older and more active than Mark's two stepchildren. He was always on the go. The stepchildren looked up to him because he was older. Linda tried to keep up with her stepson as best she could, but she had her two younger children to look after. She took them all to a water park one day for a few hours. The stepson wanted to stay all day. Her biological children, who had less stamina, wanted to leave after lunch. Linda found she suddenly could not please anyone, and she was getting no work done at home

When Mark came home from work, his son would greet him with a ball and glove. He would say, "Let's play catch." Mark did this for a few days, but after a while he tired of the hectic pace of his biological son. He preferred the more peaceful atmosphere of his stepchildren. When Mark avoided activity with his son, the burden fell on his wife. She was already worn out from taking care of her stepson all day long. Mark did not realize this.

Bray and Kelly would call Mark a "child dumper." This is a man or a woman who expects his/her spouse to "take total—or near total—responsibility for the care, nurturance, and entertainment of the visiting children."

When Linda came to Mark with this problem, a conflict arose. Mark became defensive, and then denied the fact that he was not paying attention to his child. This is a critical point. According to the authors, if this problem is not resolved it can lead to the end of the child's visits. This is another example of how problems can move up from the children to the parents.

In this case, Linda did one of the things that the authors suggest. She helped her stepson talk to his father about spending time with him. She gave him a few sentences to get him started in the conversation. It was hard for Mark to resist the direct pleas of his son, especially since the boy was only there for a month.

Let's look at another way that problems can move up from the children and cause trouble between spouses. Marge's ex-spouse is coming to take the children for the weekend. This is not one of Marge's best times. She does not like dealing with her former husband, and she does not like letting go of the children for a weekend. But there is not much she can do about it. So she grins and bears it. When the ex-spouse and the children are gone, Marge becomes irritable. With no one else around but her spouse, he has to contend with her irritability.

Don't let avoidable problems sneak up on you and

destroy your peace of mind, leaving you ready to argue. Be vigilant. See things coming, even if you do not like to look at them. Prepare for them.

I was sitting at a wedding reception with a priest and a doctor. Both men were very experienced in family life. "The husband and wife always have to make time for each other," the priest said, "even if you have to make a date with one another."

"I agree," the doctor said. "When the children were young, my wife and I contracted with a babysitter to come every Saturday night for six months at a time. And no matter what else was going on, we went out together. It has really meant a lot to us."

Perhaps we can shore up the marital relationship in the blended family by giving it all the time it needs to grow before the problems rise up from the children. Children need a lot of time and attention. But so does marriage. The love you have for one another will only help the children grow. Taking time for each other is really taking time for the family.

Another problem that the authors cite is the "just us" myth. This occurs when the couple in the blended family thinks that it is only a matter of time before all those "other people" from the past go away. Those other people include ex-spouses, the ex-spouses' relatives, and children not living in the home. Believing in this "just us" myth sets you up for failure. Of course, the other people keep coming back, and you have to deal with them as an unexpected intrusion each time. They are like unexpected guests because you denied the fact that they will return again and again. When the visit is over, you say that you are finished, but they come back again. You honestly have to admit to yourself that you will never be done with the people in your ex-spouse's past. They will always be there, so expect them. In this way you will not be disappointed every time they show up. The blended family cannot be "just us." The past has been made, and you have to live with it. Mature people accept it as a given.

Furthermore, there are some things in the past you really would not want to rule out, for example, your and/or your spouse's children from the first marriage. While they might not live with you, they will keep coming back from time to time. You need to stand ready to offer these children the hospitality of your home and your love. Make every effort to rid the family of "just us" kind of thinking.

Finding Peace

All of us want peace. We want peace of mind for ourselves and for our children. That is why we write books like this, that look at ways in which conflict can arise between a husband and wife in a blended family. We want to avoid conflict as much as we can. It is good to know how to avoid conflict and to work for peace. But one lesson that we must learn, as married people and as Christians, is that peace does not start with a cooperative spouse, or even with placid children. True peace, the peace that Christ was talking about, starts in our hearts. The only way we will bring true peace to our families and ourselves is to have the peace of Christ in our hearts.

M. Basil Pennington, a Trappist monk, tells an interesting story about Saint Benedict in his book, *A Place Apart: Monastic Prayer and Practice for Everyone* (Liguori, 1998). Benedict lived 1500 years ago and is considered the father of Western monasticism. The story goes like this.

Benedict sat at the gate of his monastery. This was his usual routine. A great calm and peacefulness surrounded Benedict. A lifetime of prayer and meditation had drawn Benedict so close to God that he remained serene and peaceful in all circumstances. But this day rumors were flowing. The rumors said that barbarians were advancing on the monastery.

Shortly after the rumors started, messengers came to the monastery. They reported that Totila, the Goth, was coming. People in the village flocked to Benedict for advice about what to do. When he gave them a message of peace, they did not listen, but fled. The monks moved prayerfully around the monastery. They shared the great peace of their father, Benedict. The mountain was deserted, except for the monks.

Then rumbling could be heard in the distance. A cloud of dust from the advancing army could be seen over the horizon. Benedict sat in his chair at the gate of the monastery. He still remained calm. The Goths came closer. Then the horde, motivated by greed, rushed forward. They thought the great monastery was full of wealth. The less confident brothers gathered inside the monastery to support Benedict with prayers.

Benedict remained peacefully at the entrance. The feared Goth, Totila, approached Benedict. When he came close to the monk, Totila was so awed by Benedict's peaceful personality and holiness that he fell at Benedict's feet. Totila left the monastery unharmed. History tells us from that day on Totila was far less cruel and more peaceful.

We cannot totally depend on elements around us to make us peaceful. On the contrary, we often have to depend on our inner peace to make things around us peaceful. In the blended family, we are dealing with not only our children and stepchildren and spouse, but also with a whole cast of others that surround the family. We cannot count on everyone to be in a good mood for us to be at peace. For reasons that we may never understand, others will have grudges, or try to sabotage our good intentions. Like Benedict, we have to make our own peace, with ourselves and with God, regardless of what is going on around us.

We can find the peace that Benedict displayed in the same way as Benedict found it. We can pray. We can try to live close to God. We can have our priorities in the right order, so that God and others come first, ahead of things. We can do this over and over, on a daily basis.

Pray for the ability to trust God. That is a tough virtue. This is one of those prayers that God is sure to answer. As you grow in trusting God, you grow in inner peace. You may not be able to turn back barbarian armies, or even an angry child, but your growth in inner peace will be a step in the right direction. Any peace you can find through prayer, you will be able to share with your family. Some quiet time everyday for prayer will put you on the road to true peace. Don't stop working at conflict resolution, or at trying to avoid conflict within your family, but help yourself along the way to all the spiritual opportunities for growth in peace and love.

CHAPTER THIRTEEN

Resources

I was not overwhelmed when I looked around for information on the blended family. If you are looking for resources on the blended family, you will have to use the word "stepfamily." I found twenty-one Internet listings under "blended family" while I found 424 listings under "stepfamily." If you are an Internet user, you might find helpful material on some of these sites and even someone to write to. Check out the information and discover which sites are relevant for you.

The *Stepfamily Association of America* (www.saafamilies.org) is worth a look if you are interested in learning more, or even looking into explaining blended families to others. This site has a magazine, a handbook, a $150.00 course with videos and CDs, and an audiocassette set on the stepfamily.

I recently visited two churches, both of which had

support group meetings for the parents of blended families listed in their bulletins. Check your parish, or if you live in a city where you have access to many churches, look around to see if any of them have support groups for the blended family. If you cannot find a support group, you might consider starting one in your parish. It doesn't take a charismatic person to start a group. A word in the bulletin, some coffee and cookies, and maybe a book that everyone agrees to read and discuss is a good start. Perhaps your pastor or family life coordinator can give you a hand at getting started. Ask your pastor who the other blended families are in the parish. Maybe he can put you in touch with them for support.

Father Anthony Palazzolo is the Advisor for the Diocesan Center for Family Life of St. Augustine. He is also the chaplain of the North American Conference of Separated and Divorced Catholics. He agrees that there is a lack of resources for the blended family and few Catholic books on the subject. In his parish, several times a year he has a workshop for the blended family. Two or three blended family couples give talks and the participants have discussions. It is a simple format. His goal is to get the blended family into the mainstream of the Church, where they belong. "They are not marginalized," Father Palazzolo says. "Who would Jesus turn away?" If you want to get a group started, Father Palazzolo is available for consultation at 904-280-5422.

Father Palazzolo advises everyone who is looking

for support for their blended family to call the Tribunal Office of their diocese. Every diocese has a fully staffed Tribunal Office that can advise you on the activities of your diocese.

The North American Conference for Separated and Divorced Catholics has a Web site (www.nacsdc.org), and you can e-mail them at nacsdc@pinetel.com. This Web site will be a huge help to those who feel that they are somehow marginal members of the Church because they are divorced. The Conference's address is P.O. Box 360, Richland, Oregon 97870. You can reach them by phone at 541-893-6089.

If reading is your forte, try looking up "stepfamily" on Amazon's or Barnes and Noble's Web sites. You can browse through their listings to see what appeals to you. Some of the books I cited in my writing may be of interest. *Stepfamilies* by Bray and Kelly, while not a Catholic book, is an interesting book, but it may tell you more than you want to know. *Making Peace in Your Stepfamily* is a little simpler, but it is also not Catholic. The Catholic books in this area are limited. The one Catholic book I cited was M. Basil Pennington's book, *A Place Apart*. This is excellent spiritual reading. It will introduce you to the way monks live and how any person, even in a busy blended family, can seek peace in life. While it is not a book on the blended family, it is a spiritual book that a member of the blended family can feel confident about. Its high ideals are extremely practical.

Afterword

This book has focused on many things to make your vocation more meaningful to you and your spouse and children. The book attempts to describe what kinds of things go on inside of you and your blended family, how parents and children adjust, and even how some families live out the experience of the blended family. I have tried to look at all the members of the blended family, even those on the outside, in order to help you avoid conflict. But that still leaves at least one very important thing yet to be done.

At the end of his book—the one that contained the story of Benedict and the Goths—Father Pennington writes that we can wish we were more holy and prayerful, but it is never enough to just wish. We have to put our wishes into action. That is what remains for the readers of this book. We may wish we had more understanding of our blended family.

We may wish we saw our daily tasks more as a vibrant part of our vocation. We may wish that we had enough inner peace to help avoid at least some conflicts. But that is not enough. We have to put our wishes into action.

Father Pennington offers his readers three steps that apply to the readers' of this book. *First*, ask yourself what needs to be done. For example, what is missing that keeps your family from being at peace? *Second*, ask yourself how you are going to accomplish this. In other words, how will you bring about the peace you desire? *Finally*, how are you going to get the support you need?

For example, you say, "I want inner peace so that I can be more patient with my spouse and children." Second, make a modest resolution about what you will do to attain it. You may say, "I will pray every morning for five minutes," or, "I will read the Bible for five minutes each evening." Start small, so you can keep your resolution. Third, look first of all to your spouse for support. Tell him or her what you would like to accomplish, and what you are going to do to accomplish it. Also, pray for support to accomplish your desire and to help to your family.

These three questions will help you put your good intentions into action. I used peace as an example, but it can be anything you want to accomplish in your blended family. Take one small thing you would like to accomplish at a time. Maybe you want to not only do something for your family, but also to do something for other blended families. Father Palazzolo thinks the blended family can be helped tremendously by quality affordable day care run by the church. "What a great way to evangelize," he says.

One woman in our parish, with a few of her friends, started Mothers' Morning Out. It is a simple program. The parent drops off the children one day a week, from 8 a.m. to noon.

Parenting classes for the families in general and blended families specifically can be a big help, even, indirectly, a support group.

We all can benefit from marriage preparation, whether we're getting married for the first time or not. Special marital preparation for people going into blended families would be a good way to help them become aware of their unique vocation and give them some support. Several parishes could combine in this effort.

Whether you are working to improve your own blended family or a group of blended families, remember, living and loving in a blended family is a special vocation. You have a call from God, and God is with you. As Trappist monk Thomas Merton said, God will never leave us to face our perils alone.

About the Author

R alph Ranieri has been a licensed clinical social worker for thirty years. A husband, father, and grandfather, Ranieri has also been active in Marriage Encounter and Cursillo. He has published many articles, pamphlets, and books over the years. Recent Liguori titles include Liguori Kids' Heroes pamphlets *Blessed Teresa of Calcutta* and *Pope John Paul II;* teen issues in *Staying Cool When You're Freaking Out;* adult spirituality in *Growing in Wisdom and Grace;* and parenting issues in *Connecting: Now That Your Children Are Adults.*